DISPLACING THEORY THROUGH THE GLOBAL SOUTH

Cultural Inquiry

EDITED BY CHRISTOPH F. E. HOLZHEY
AND MANUELE GRAGNOLATI

The series 'Cultural Inquiry' is dedicated to exploring how diverse cultures can be brought into fruitful rather than pernicious confrontation. Taking culture in a deliberately broad sense that also includes different discourses and disciplines, it aims to open up spaces of inquiry, experimentation, and intervention. Its emphasis lies in critical reflection and in identifying and highlighting contemporary issues and concerns, even in publications with a historical orientation. Following a decidedly cross-disciplinary approach, it seeks to enact and provoke transfers among the humanities, the natural and social sciences, and the arts. The series includes a plurality of methodologies and approaches, binding them through the tension of mutual confrontation and negotiation rather than through homogenization or exclusion.

Christoph F. E. Holzhey is the Founding Director of the ICI Berlin Institute for Cultural Inquiry. Manuele Gragnolati is Professor of Italian Literature at the Sorbonne Université in Paris and Associate Director of the ICI Berlin.

DISPLACING THEORY THROUGH THE GLOBAL SOUTH

EDITED BY
IRACEMA DULLEY
ÖZGÜN EYLÜL İŞCEN

ISBN (Hardcover): 978-3-96558-066-4
ISBN (Paperback): 978-3-96558-067-1
ISBN (PDF): 978-3-96558-068-8
ISBN (EPUB): 978-3-96558-069-5

Cultural Inquiry, 29
ISSN (Print): 2627-728X
ISSN (Online): 2627-731X

Bibliographical Information of the German National Library
The German National Library lists this publication in the Deutsche
Nationalbibliografie (German National Bibliography); detailed
bibliographic information is available online at http://dnb.d-nb.de.

© 2024 ICI Berlin Press

Cover design: Studio Bens. Based on a paper collage by Claudia Peppel,
Sudden Flash of Memory, 2019, 21 x 29.7 cm.

In Europe, volumes are printed by Lightning Source UK Ltd., Milton
Keynes, UK. See the final page for further details.

Digital editions can be viewed and downloaded freely at:
https://doi.org/10.37050/ci-29.

ICI Berlin Press is an imprint of
ICI gemeinnütziges Institut für Cultural Inquiry Berlin GmbH
Christinenstr. 18/19, Haus 8
D-10119 Berlin
publishing@ici-berlin.org
www.ici-berlin.org

Contents

Introduction
Displacing Theory: Berlin Notes
IRACEMA DULLEY AND ÖZGÜN EYLÜL İŞCEN

How is it possible to theorize not only on the so-called Global South, but also in, from, and through it? This question involves reflecting on the institutional, disciplinary, and rhetorical devices that shape the production of theory, as much as on geopolitical inequalities and the entanglement of knowledge production and imperialism. This joint collection results both from our commitment to the long-standing critique of colonialism, imperialism, and Eurocentrism, and from our inquiries into where and how to move from there.

As Berlin-based researchers and practitioners invested in both theorization and a specific historical and geopolitical context, we recurrently face the frustration of having our work either reduced to the particularity of its context or subsumed into Eurocentric generalizations. In this vein, we propose to reflect on the following questions: How are our theoretical affinities transformed through contexts in

1

the so-called Global South? How can we make our work relevant to a larger audience beyond a particular region or a field defined in terms of area studies? What are possible strategies to present the theoretical impact of our work despite its constant peripheralization as a case study? What affordances can certain disciplines and institutions offer to tackle such theoretical and methodological challenges?

What appears as the universal often involves a gesture of generalization that flattens and dominates the particular, predominantly from a Eurocentric perspective. We wish to simultaneously unsettle the very distinction between the general and the particular that underlies asymmetrical claims to universality and retain the claim to the universal that makes theorization generative and relevant. How can one maintain a critique of the Eurocentric gaze without falling into the traps of ethnocentrism, which ends up posing one's particularity as a universal, or cultural relativism, which leads to discursive and political ambivalence regarding the local manifestations of capitalist imperial violence? What methodologies can be employed to expand, if not transform, our understandings of the universal? How can one relate discourse to positionality without implying that the position occupied by a subject is equivalent to the totality of discourse one can produce from that specific place?

This book results from a series of encounters in Berlin. On this basis, we reached out to scholars working within a wide range of fields and regions, and some of these scholars became contributors to this collection, in which we jointly address the above-mentioned questions. Our first encounter took place in a monthly reading group in which we engaged with and discussed the works of scholars who propose to both theorize and reflect on areas of the world that are now said to be located in the Global South without reducing such areas to sites where theory is to be applied or tested. At ICI Berlin, we organized a public workshop titled *Theorizing Through the Global South*, which took place from 10–11 March 2022 and was followed by a publication workshop on 11 November 2022.[1]

This collection of essays is the product of the vibrant conversation we developed on all these occasions. As such, it embodies a collective nature and the situatedness of our project. It does not intend to be exhaustive. Rather, it aims to discuss and challenge the relationship between the production of theory as a form of generalization and the tendency to relegate locations in the Global South, as well as the intellectuals who are associated with it, to the role of either suppliers of raw material for abstraction produced in the Global North or consumers of its final products. As explored by some of the position papers that compose this volume, this power imbalance depends on relations that are both material and symbolic.

Collaboration and dialogue are core features of this enterprise because we believe they are central to the task of undoing such divides. Yet, dialogue does not always mean agreement. Thus, not only consensus but also dissonance is to be found among the positions taken by the various authors that compose this collection. Titles have also been the matter of much discussion among us. The title of the workshop we organized in March, *Theorizing Through the Global South*, was an object of opposition for different reasons: the centrality ascribed to theory; Global South as a designation; the possible implication that theory is something distinct from its objects. Such attention is given to the title because it not only announces but also performs the paradox that drives our discussion. What do we mean

---

1   See 'Theorizing Through the Global South', workshop, ICI Berlin, 10–11 March 2022 <https://doi.org/10.25620/e220310>.

when we say 'theorizing'? What do we mean with 'Global South'? Or, as some contributors bring up, aren't these only to be thought of in the plural — knowledges, Global Souths? These questions are all interrelated.

The concept of the Global South is compelling because it simultaneously implies global and local scales of theorization. In its localization, this concept hints at the particular that is usually associated with the empirical, whereas the idea of the global points to the attempt at universalization. Yet, the Global South is thought of in relation to something, and that implicit something is the site from which theory is usually thought to be produced: Europe, the North, the West, or the like. Another problem with the concept of a Global South is that the process through which such an entity is constituted depends on hierarchizations and reifications that end up reproducing power asymmetries within knowledge production.

As we aim to analyse such power relations, it is important to keep in mind that they also shape the ways in which we produce what we here call theory (for lack of a better word). In this sense, our title poses a paradox, which is the paradox that is posed whenever one gestures towards generalization and simultaneously reveals the contingent, provisional, and unfinished character of this gesture. We thus invite you to dwell with us on the paradoxical position that consists of undoing the opposition between the theoretical and the empirical, the North and the South, the general and the particular, while still having recourse to the oppositional languages and infrastructures in which our thoughts and actions take place.

Our new title, *Displacing Theory*, highlights the work of transformation that results from a reassessment of the relationship between particularization and generalization. This reassessment occurs when one proposes to theorize without subsuming places that have been the object of colonialism, imperialism, and extractive capitalism to a reductive, Eurocentric gaze. From this displacement of theory, replacements and new emplacements ensue — a process that happens in space and time and involves collaboration. This is why we have chosen to think of the 'Global South' as modified by the adjective 'so-called'. In so doing, we recognize the structural inequalities between the so-called Global North and the so-called Global South while at the same time marking the limited ability of such designations to describe anything that has actuality on the ground. Moreover, as our title highlights, theory is produced not only *on* something but also *through* and *from* it.

Ideally, we would like to extend the collaboration between theoretical and empirical investigation to our situatedness as both the producers and the subjects of theory. Indeed, this trajectory motivated our invitation to Berlin-based scholars to delve into this endeavour with us because our questions and methods also derive from the concrete sites in which we produce knowledge. In this regard, we are committed to tackling more pragmatic issues concerning our practice, such as developing networks, resources, and strategies within academia or the realm of cultural production at large. Each locality and each positionality come with distinct possibilities and challenges that reconfigure our working and living conditions.

For instance, we are often expected to work on specific 'safe' and 'valuable' themes and often discouraged, if not prevented, from working outside these thematic zones. These repressive mechanisms operate through devices that are sometimes implicit, such as funding and visibility structures, and sometimes explicit, such as institutional and racial discrimination, censorship, and peer pressure. Needless to say, this happens within and beyond academia.

Moreover, as a collectivity mostly composed of immigrants living in Berlin, we often face precarity due to the instability of jobs, housing, and immigration status, sometimes accompanied by the impossibility or the obligation of returning to our so-called home countries.

Some of us, coming from, working within, and allying with targeted communities, are confronted with anti-immigrant, anti-Palestinian, and anti-black sentiments, whether official, public, or implicit, that make themselves apparent in the cultural and political landscapes of contemporary Germany. Even though there have been increasing efforts towards decolonizing cultural and educational settings, these initiatives usually fall short of confronting Germany's colonial history and presence, which is an essential task if one is to effectively address processes of repatriation, restitution, and reparation. Still, the diverse communities of Berlin help us learn from and partake in each other's struggles within the city and parts of the world to which we feel that we belong in one way or another. As described above, what we mean by theorization also entails embracing different corners of the city that manifest multiple ways of overcoming the divides we tackle in this book.

Many contributors to this volume address the theoretical and political possibilities and challenges of their intersectional positionality, producing knowledge on and through the Global South while placed in Berlin, Europe, or the Global North at large. Some of them take this task as part of an agenda for decolonizing knowledge production. In other words, they aim at contesting colonial regimes of knowledge, which hierarchize, marginalize, and devalue certain modes and sites of theorization, while embracing the relational and processual nature of intellectual work, which is to say, a pluriversal method of thinking.

In her contribution, Michela Coletta introduces the idea of 'entangled ecologies' to attend to the cross-hemispheric histories of extractive capitalism that have shaped the politics of knowledge production. To this end, she engages with decolonial thinkers and environmental movements unfolding in Latin America as much as with her professional and intellectual crossings. On the one hand, Coletta unsettles the predominant conceptual order, which has led to the North-South division and other dichotomies, such as indigeneity and modernity, in the first place. On the other hand, she offers more complex models and methodologies for mapping (the history of) community-based practices of knowledge-making that are attentive to the increasingly complex interconnections across human and non-human worlds. Ultimately, through her investment in entanglement, she calls for non-anthropocentric alliances in order to address the planetary crises we face today.

In Mahmoud Al-Zayed's contribution, we witness a similar emphasis on tackling the urgencies of our times, such as mass displacements due to the ongoing imperial wars, and reframing decolonial critique as a situated practice. According to Al-Zayed, each location generates different sets of problems and questions that motivate varied modes of decoloniality, which is to say, decolonialities. Without romanticizing the bitter experience of forced displacement, and while drawing upon decolonial thinkers living in exile, including himself, Al-Zayed engages with the plurality of thought embedded within the exilic intellectual formation that can potentially undo colonial forms of knowledge-making and being in the world. Indeed, for him, the critical potential of exilic consciousness resides in its possibility to generate a pluriversal method of thinking that can unsettle various colonial epistemic forms of monolingualism and monohumanism that rely on the self-sufficiency of thought.

This very exilic condition, with all the challenges and possibilities embedded within it, also comes up in Şirin Fulya Erensoy's contribution on the feminist artistic landscape emerging in Berlin, with its growing, diverse migrant community. Erensoy, by reflecting on homemaking practices in exile, explores how women* artists challenge the imposed notions — borders and boundaries of exclusion/inclusion — that come along with their migrant status within the city. Thus, she shows us how feminisms from the Global South decentralize claims to truth by taking the means of production into their own hands. By engaging with the recent protests that have unfolded in Berlin in solidarity with the feminist revolution in Iran, she simultaneously exposes the limits of such mobilizations whenever they do not embrace intersectionality and proposes to invest in feminist artistic practices that destabilize exclusionary politics as they bridge theory and practice.

While focusing on the specific case of knowledge production in and about Iran, Firoozeh Farvardin and Nader Talebi point out the risk of reproducing a Northern perspective as one attempts to produce knowledge on and through the Global South(s). Whenever this is the case, the effects are cognitive suppression, further peripheralization, or even recolonization of the South(s). Farvardin and Talebi emphasize the long-lasting effects of methodological nationalism and its political effects, such as in the adoption of nativist discourses historically connected to the 'Islamic' Revolution by scholars focusing on the Global South(s) and in area studies concerning Iran. To avoid these effects, Farvardin and Talebi draw upon the politics of scale in their critique of the power asymmetries underlying the hierarchization of Northern and Southern sites of knowledge production and claim that one should acknowledge the diverse particularities of these sites and communities, which are often flattened within the seemingly coherent categories of nation or region. Eventually, the contribution of Farvardin and Talebi demonstrates the significance of prioritizing the very site from and on which knowledge is produced, Iran in this case. Indeed, they shed light on the dialectical nature of the mediation between there (Iran) and here (Germany), which includes paying heed to one's in-betweenness as a Berlin-based immigrant scholar.

Speaking to the problem of mediation (e.g. between here and there) as inherently part of any attempt at representation as well as theorization, Iracema Dulley and Juliana M. Streva question the politics, if not the possibility, of speaking for others, the ultimate colonial gesture through which authority is claimed. As they engage in a dialogue among themselves and with Trinh T. Minh-ha's idea and practice of 'speaking nearby', Dulley and Streva demonstrate how, in Western academia, the acts of reading and writing have granted authority to the figure of the author as the knowledge producer par excellence — for Trinh the 'voice of knowledge'.[2] In return, they invest in liberating the act of speaking-writing from the colonial structures of othering and ownership that are continually reinscribed by disciplinary, authoritarian systems of knowledge. Thus, Dulley and Streva invite us to speak, think, and listen nearby, which ultimately relies on the recognition that the language of others, in whatever form, remains opaque to us. Inspired by an ethics and epistemology of

---

2   See Trinh T. Minh-ha, '"Speaking Nearby": A Conversation with Trinh T. Minh-ha', *Visual Anthropology Review*, 8.1 (1992), pp. 82–91 and Trinh T. Minh-ha, *Woman, Native, Other: Writing Postcoloniality and Feminism* (Bloomington: Indiana University Press, 1989), p. 63.

fugitivity, the authors argue that in striving for dialogue, there is the possibility of displacing theory and unsettling colonial legacies.

Displacing the assigned authority of the researcher, especially within an anthropological fieldwork setting and all the colonial registers it thrives upon, Iracema Dulley and Frederico Santos dos Santos tackle the relationship between naming and social positionality. To this end, they offer a comparative analysis of Dulley's being designated as *branca* and *ocindele* in Angola and Santos's being interpellated as *toubab* in Senegal. In so doing, they explore how thinking of the intersections between race, class, and religion can be relevant to situate the positions from which ethnographic research is produced. Yet, since such broad categories frequently do not find equivalents in the context of fieldwork, understanding positionality in context involves paying attention to how these categories are displaced in the process of their translation into the languages in which designators usually generalized in terms of race, class, religion, etc. are locally expressed — in the cases addressed here, Wolof, Portuguese, and Umbundu. Thus, while arguing for the political and ethical relevance of taking intersectional positionality into account, Dulley and Santos also highlight the need to listen to one's interlocutors and pay heed to local forms of expressing relations of power that challenge such pre-established categories.

In continuity with these vernacular experiences of moving across multiple sites and languages, other contributions in this volume engage with historically situated examples that dissolve the prescribed roles of intellectuals from the Global South/North. Instead, these contributions demonstrate how to perform what Coletta calls entangled ecologies of knowledge, which complicate the history of thought — in the cases addressed here, Marxist theory and Radical Psychiatry. With reference to the Marx Seminars at the University of São Paulo between the late 1950s and early 1960s, Bernardo Bianchi examines, by means of a confrontation with temporal as much as spatial dualisms, the creation of a specific tradition in the social sciences. He argues that the development of this new perspective must be understood in terms of its efforts to rethink Marx but also, and more importantly, of the need of Brazilian intellectuals to rethink Brazil's place in the shifting world system. Following this thread, Bianchi analyses Roberto Schwarz's work as paradigmatic for understanding the centrality of the concept of the periphery in these discussions that account for a specific moment in the history of postcolonial and decolonial studies.

Marlon Miguel's contribution, in turn, focuses on the work of Brazilian psychiatrist Nise da Silveira, a pioneer who introduced artistic tools into her work with her patients, especially those diagnosed as psychotic. Miguel argues that Nise, as she is widely known by first name in Brazil, produced a deeply innovative and reflective practice as she engaged with a variety of European psychiatrists, psychoanalysts, and thinkers within and through her situatedness in Brazil. Her work resonates in particular with French Institutional Psychotherapy, as well as with Frantz Fanon's psychiatric work in Algeria, but also differs from them in that she places art at the core of her clinical method and radically opposes medicalized approaches. According to Miguel, in the contemporary context of a renewed organicist vision of mental disorders, novel perspectives on current clinical debates could be gained from inverting the marginalization of figures from the Global South, such as Nise da Silveira, and from considering the history of Brazilian psychiatry and psychoanalysis.

European traditions of canonization that flatten and marginalize some historical figures of intellectual thought are also questioned in Kata Katz's think piece. With the provocative (working) title 'Kill your Darlings', Katz explores what it means to exist in a culture of idols by questioning the universalistic practice of canonization. To this end, along with other contributors who rely on a feminist perspective to develop their critical yet creative analyses, she builds upon feminist praxis to denounce the (most often male) genius-based, self-contained understanding of creativity and success that is often found in contemporary scientific research. Instead, she engages with several thinkers that could make up a 'masterclass' while proposing to go beyond a male-thinkers-dominated curriculum in order to make room for the voices of plurality and collective thinking. Demonstrating what she argues for in her own writing style, Katz presents a case for cultivating cultures of failure within and at the edges of academia.

While adopting a similar experimental style, some contributions situate the volume within the context in which it came into being, thereby dissolving the distance between here and there in terms of both space and time. For instance, Ana Carolina Schveitzer invests in rendering Germany's hidden yet omnipresent colonial past visible by means of a walk through Berlin, during which she highlights places related to this part of German history. Schveitzer argues that even though there is an increased interest in decolonial praxis within Berlin-based cultural and educational settings, the persistence of such efforts and their implications within larger society are hard to assess in advance. In response, her contribution builds a thread of several references to colonialism spread through the city while engaging with initiatives that seek to contest this complicated history and make visible their presence today as more than mere residues of the past. Ultimately, Schveitzer critically reflects on the possibilities and challenges of the ongoing struggles for historical reparation, which will increasingly occupy the cultural landscape of Germany with the growth of public awareness and collective mobilization.

Finally, the volume ends with Bruna Martins Coelho's intriguing contribution: a letter addressed to the researchers of the South located in the North. Resorting to concepts drawn from feminist, decolonial, postcolonial, and post-structuralist literature as well as from Marx-inspired sociological literature on labour, Martins Coelho indicates many of the impasses related to the processes through which labour relations are made precarious in academia. In her summary of the setbacks of academic life in the world at large and in Germany in particular, the prosaic tone of her narrative reminds us of how quotidian and banal aspects of precarity are interconnected with its structural character. In doing so, she shows how researchers from the Global South experience a further layer of precarization while based in the North, even though some convert this situatedness into a status currency when they go back to where they come from, often in the face of worsened economic and political instability.

As this outline demonstrates, the contributions to this collection address the varied issues our dialogues have raised and contain in themselves the dialogical nature of our collaboration, sometimes even in their writing style. Since the current volume proceeded through regular meetings and conversations, it presents our, the editors', primary research networks in Berlin. For, as far as the relationship between theorization and the so-called Global South is concerned, most of our collaborators work on contexts within Latin America and the Middle East. Still, alongside some other contributors to this volume, we would like to underline the in-betweenness of our scholarship and research sites, blurring our belonging to any region or research paradigm. Indeed, we are critical of the titling, grouping, and mapping that operate in representational terms and reduce us to commodified and profitable labels.

We see this volume as a toolbox that came out of our particular yet collective, as well as persistent, experience of working together. This collection thus gives material form to a joint effort to tackle the ethical, political, and intellectual questions that arise whenever one attempts to both theorize and work through places situated in the so-called Global South. We would like to thank all the contributors, workshop participants, ICI Berlin fellows, staff and the ICI Berlin Press team that have made this journey possible, and we are happy to invite you to take part in it.

History of Knowledge through the Global South
A Case for Entangled Ecologies
MICHELA COLETTA

LOCATING KNOWLEDGE

When researching the history of epistemic production originating outside of the Euro-Anglo sphere, I am faced with geographical, theoretical, and methodological challenges. What does it mean, for example, to think from or through specific localities like Latin America, Africa, or Asia? Is this a valid question in the first place? How does one deal with established historiographical binary categories such as modern and traditional, as well as western and non-western?[1] What methodologies are needed when, for

---

1   In this essay, I have used uncapitalized versions of all regional terms, such as west/western, south/southern, and so forth, to acknowledge the power dynamics that determine the changeable geopolitical significance of their usage.

example, studying multilingual sources? What are the implications of using the global south framework alongside disciplinary approaches such as global history?

These are some of the questions that I bear in mind in my work as an intellectual historian studying the production of eco-social knowledge in Latin America as part of the global dynamics of violence, resistance, and exchange. The multiplicity of localities that have shaped my intellectual self adds further complexity. After deeply formative schooling in the Latin and Greek classics alongside the canon of western philosophy and literature in my southern Italian hometown, I studied and later researched the literature and history of Latin America, mostly in UK academia with a few south-bound turns along the way. How does my own intellectual locatedness as a southern European producing scholarship in the north further complicate this picture?

There is, however, a question that pre-empts all the previous ones: What is considered knowledge, and who is deemed able to produce it? Acknowledging the title of cultural critic and literature scholar Hamid Dabashi's book, *Can Non-Europeans Think?*,[2] in the brief discussion that follows, I will reflect on the significance of using the category of the global south to reconfigure the history of knowledge, which continues to largely coincide with the history of western thought and western science. I use 'knowledge' here to include diverse ways of relating to the world that may not fall neatly within the methodological boundaries of disciplined epistemologies.

While it is relevant, and even urgent, to theorize from and about the global south, it is also necessary to bear in mind the geopolitical nature of the category, which

---

2   Hamid Dabashi, *Can Non-Europeans Think?* With a foreword by Walter
     Mignolo (London: Zed Books, 2015).

overlaps with those countries that until recently were grouped among the developing or underdeveloped economies. Therefore, even though I see this as a productive paradigm shift that has already given rise to mould-breaking works, I argue for a framework that can grasp the cross-hemispheric histories of extractive capitalism and how both colonial violence and anticolonial resistance have shaped knowledge-making. Reading these dynamics as 'entangled ecologies', I suggest, would enable us to ask better and deeper questions about the increasingly complex interconnections across human and nonhuman worlds in processes such as environmental, economic, and financial extractivisms, human and nonhuman migrations, and ecological and cultural loss. Perhaps this perspective leads to a more fitting version of my preliminary question: What modes of knowledge production do we need to cultivate in an age of climate breakdown and mass extinction?

WHERE IS THE GLOBAL SOUTH?

In the foreword to Dabashi's book, Argentine decolonial theorist Walter Mignolo suggests that it is necessary to undiscipline thinking because western philosophy is not the only way to think.[3] This seems to be a productive reflection that bears not only on the content of knowledge (what is worth thinking and theorizing about) but also, and perhaps even more importantly, on its methods (how thought can be accessed and processed to produce plural avenues for interpreting and creating complex interactions across multiple worlds). For example, I have recently explored community-based practices of knowing-with in Colombia's Caribbean region that unsettle the body-mind

---

3   Walter Mignolo, 'Foreword: Yes, We Can', in Dabashi, *Can Non-Europeans Think?*, pp. viii–xlii (pp. xi–xii).

dichotomy central to dominant western epistemologies and encourage the cultivation of alternative methodologies.[4] Theorizing through the global south is a crucial step towards the urgent task of undertaking an 'ecology of knowledge' in order both to acknowledge erasures and to reveal plural knowledge systems.[5] In this respect, the framework of entangled ecologies that I am proposing further emphasizes the planetary interconnections underlying knowledge-making.

The first step is to consider the geopolitical significance of the category of the global south as it results from its institutional constitution. The term 'south' was already circulating in the 1970s and was relatively well-established by the 1980s as a means to roughly indicate 'Third World' countries and to mark a north-south distinction. The key document that validated the global south as an identifiable geoeconomic region was the 2004 United Nations report 'Forging a Global South', and it did so largely in terms of economic development.[6] Although geographically ubiquitous, the term combines the north-south polarization with an increasingly integrated market economy. Many scholars claim that the unevenness shaping the material and discursive conditions that constitute the global south should

4   Michela Coletta, 'A World without Objects: Epistemic Bordering for a Transformative Future', *FORMA — A Journal of Latin American Criticism & Theory*, 2.1 (2023), pp. 109–31.

5   Boaventura de Sousa Santos, *Epistemologies of the South: Justice Against Epistemicide* (New York: Routledge, 2014).

6   Michela Coletta and Malayna Raftopoulos, 'Counter-Hegemonic Narratives and the Politics of Plurality: Problematising Global Environmental Governance from Latin America through the Case of Bolivia', *Iberoamericana — Nordic Journal of Latin American and Caribbean Studies*, 47.1 (2018), pp. 108–17 <https://doi.org/10.16993/iberoamericana.429>; Arif Dirlik, 'Global South: Predicament and Promise', *The Global South*, 1.1 (2007), pp. 12–23; United Nations Development Programme, Special issue 'Forging a Global South', United Nations Day for South-South Cooperation, 19 December 2004.

be considered from the perspective of continued western imperialism.[7] While this new geopolitical assemblage disarranges the traditional boundaries of earlier world-system divisions, it once again masks those sets of historic relations instead of replacing them. The global south coincides with those countries previously under the umbrella of the underdeveloped and developing world.

While it is, then, critical to acknowledge new possibilities of agency whereby 'the global south names the places where decolonial emancipations are taking place and where new horizons of life are emerging',[8] it remains challenging to overcome the extractive economic and epistemic relations that underpin the north-south division. Consequently, as Dabashi claims, we must be wary of continuing to uphold stark distinctions, because '[t]his "we" is no longer we folks in the global South, for some of us have migrated to the global North [...], [and it] includes all those disenfranchised by the global operation of capital whether in the north or south [...]'.[9] I reflect on this statement as a migrant academic working in a Global History Department in Berlin, which encourages me to envisage rewriting the history of knowledge through and from the global south as a vital project of epistemic reparation towards the wider undertaking of what I call 'entangled ecologies'.

Thinking through 'entangled ecologies' is a tool for countering the existing conceptual order, which has led

---

7   *Handbook of Transnational Governance: New Institutions and Innovations*, ed. by David Held and Thomas Hale (Cambridge: Polity Press, 2011).

8   Caroline Levander and Walter Mignolo, 'Introduction: The Global South and World Dis/Order', *The Global South*, 5.1 (2011), pp. 1–11 (pp. 4–5) <https://doi.org/10.2979/globalsouth.5.1.1>.

9   Dabashi, *Can Non-Europeans Think?*, p. 43.

to the north-south division in the first place. Postcolonial studies have uncovered the continued material and intellectual dependency of post-independence countries as well as the local genealogies of universalist worldviews. However, postcolonial scholars, having been trained in the same methodologies from the humanities and social sciences, have been largely drawing upon the same theories whose long-lasting effects they propose to debunk. In contrast, over the last few decades, global south intellectual movements have been much more closely involved with social and environmental struggles than before. For example, the Latin American decolonial turn initiated by the Modernity/Coloniality group in the late 1990s has an activist component, which, while not being an advantage in and by itself, marks a significant shift that has helped to reposition cultural production at the centre of political change.[10]

While participating in and building on the much-needed work of south-centred scholarship, I suggest that 'entangled ecologies' of knowledge are necessary to account for south-north contaminations in view of processes of coloniality that are increasingly planetary through a convergence of multiple lines of extractivism, which are not only environmental and economic but also financial and technological.[11] Therefore, understanding the realm of knowledge production through entangled ecologies refers, firstly, to the historical approach of entangled history, which has already addressed the limits of postcolonial theory by drawing attention to the interconnections between

---

10   The extent to which the academy is co-opting and disciplining grassroots methodologies is an important element of the critiques directed to Latin American decolonial scholars.

11   Sandro Mezzadra and Brett Neilson, 'On the Multiple Frontiers of Extraction: Excavating Contemporary Capitalism', *Cultural Studies*, 31.2–3 (2017), pp. 185–204 <https://doi.org/10.1080/09502386.2017.1303425>.

and across societies. Secondly, it evokes the idea that the separation between humans and nature is no longer tenable and that new exchanges between organic and inorganic matter have reached an unprecedented scale. Let us think, for example, of how plastics are transported by rivers, follow ocean currents, and are ingested by fish and water birds. The conception of knowledge-building processes as partaking in complex relations involving human and nonhuman encounters resonates with what Karen Barad calls 'posthumanist performativity'.[12] In order to address the dangerously unbalanced politics of knowledge and, as importantly, to account for the political, economic, and ecological interconnections that exist in knowledge production, we need to look at the global south in more expansive terms.

'The interstitial South is the otherness within the North; therefore, it can be defined essentially in relation to the North rather than in absolute terms', writes Marco Armiero in his analysis of the environmental campaigns against waste management in Italy's southern region of Campania.[13] 'The interstitial South', he continues, 'is, of course, a matter of money; the poor are everywhere, even within the rich societies of the so-called developed countries. The urban space reproduces segregation and social stratification, creating the interstitial South of ghettoes.'[14] Armiero's image of the south as an interstitial space that

---

12   Karen Barad, 'Posthumanist Performativity: Toward an Understanding of How Matter Comes to Matter', *Signs: Journal of Women in Culture and Society*, 28.3 (2003), pp. 801–31 <https://doi.org/10.1086/345321>.

13   Marco Armiero, 'Is There an Indigenous Knowledge in the Global North? Re/Inventing Local Knowledge and Communities in the Struggles over Garbage and Incinerators in Campania, Italy', *Estudos de Sociologia*, 1.20 (2014) <https://periodicos.ufpe.br/revistas/revsocio/article/view/235511> [accessed 16 September 2022].

14   Ibid.

opens gaps of economic poverty and social marginality through the north helps convey the idea of the porous and fragmented nature of geographical divisions such as north and south. My question is, then, what this means for epistemic production. In my research on Andean and Amazonian paradigms of 'Living Well' (*Buen Vivir*), I find global history methods useful for looking at the long-standing, and often violence-driven, intersections within and across cultures located as either 'indigenous' or 'western'. How should these north-south entanglements traversing local, regional, and global scales be addressed when studying knowledge production?

ENTANGLED ECOLOGIES OF KNOWLEDGE

For Dilip Menon, 'doing theory from the Global South stems from the exigent demand for decolonizing knowledge and developing a conceptual vocabulary from traditions of located intellection.'[15] This focus on the locatedness of intellectual production stands out in relation to the global dominance of Euro-American episteme. Menon addresses this issue by framing it largely in terms of (un)translatability: 'Not all conceptions are translatable across cultures and this gives us occasion to think about the hubris of the universal assumptions of our academic practices.'[16] This idea of (un)translatability reminds us of the relevance of knowledge that arises from specific human and ecological environments. It is also critical for enabling a fuller — if never complete — validation of lost or marginalized cultural practices in an attempt to account for those experiences of violence that

---

15   *Changing Theory: Concepts from the Global South*, ed. by Dilip M. Menon (Milton Park: Routledge, 2022), p. 24.

16   Ibid, p. 26.

are neither 'indigenous' nor 'modern', such as in the case of the Caribbean.[17] From this perspective, addressing the entangled ecologies of knowledge production complicates binary systems such as global north and global south by revealing those 'miscegenated genealogies'.[18]

Recently, I have revisited the notion of the peripheral as a prolific epistemic state through the work of Aymara-Bolivian sociologist Silvia Rivera Cusicanqui. I have proposed the framework of *epistemic bordering* to theorize the expansion of the peripheral condition of living across multiple worlds at once.[19] As a scholar who has migrated from the south to the north of Europe and mingled with communities of migrant scholars, I have lived and worked through those economic, social, and intellectual intersections across such geopolitical divides. Bordering knowledge also means allowing for intellectual and linguistic impurity, contamination between the spheres of theory and practice, and un-disciplinarity. 'The wandering gaze', writes Rivera Cusicanqui, 'understood as peripheral and fully awake to its environment, has the potential of being all-encompassing and is capable of relating at once to itself and to everything else', thereby 'transcend[ing] the anthropocentric nature of the social'.[20] This concept of the peripheral draws from anticolonial indigenous resistance as much as from Walter Benjamin's writings on history and modernity, especially given their critique of the modernist notion of linear movement. While this notion is governed

---

17   Malcolm Ferdinand, *Decolonial Ecology: Thinking from the Caribbean World*, trans. by Anthony Paul Smith (Cambridge: Polity Press, 2022).

18   Menon, *Changing Theory*, p. 11.

19   Coletta, 'A World without Objects'.

20   Silvia Rivera Cusicanqui, *Un mundo ch'ixi es posible. Ensayos desde un presente en crisis* (Buenos Aires: Tinta Limón, 2018), p. 41. Unless otherwise noted, all translations are my translation.

by the principle of exclusion, which leaves behind what does not conform to its forward direction, the peripheral perspective is anticolonial insofar as it is multidirectional and multilayered.

An entangled ecology of knowledge helps us to address Menon's central question about the temporality of knowledge production in the global north: 'What is lost when one reflects with the social theory of modernity, and its abbreviated sense of time, that creates a timeline from the Enlightenment in Europe?'[21] Entangled ecologies account for multiple temporalities that coexist, as the periphery is no longer a geographically identifiable place but enmeshed within planetary relationships of material, technological, digital, financial, and human mining. Peripheries travel by following the routes of the financial exploitation of human labour or by being connected through the carbon offset schemes that big polluters like oil and gas corporations use to compensate for their emissions.[22] However, through these capitalocentric dynamics of coloniality, multidirectional systems of interactions emerge, as well as possibilities to imagine alternative ways of building assemblages that flourish from the coexistence of difference.[23] For example, in reformulating the temporality of modernity, Rivera Cusicanqui advocates for the 'project of long temporality' of what she calls 'indigenous modernity'.

---

21 Menon, *Changing Theory*, p. 10

22 Josh Lederman, 'Corporations Are Turning to Forest Credits in the Race to Go "Carbon-Neutral." Advocates Worry about "Greenwashing"', *NBC News*, 5 December 2021 <https://www.nbcnews.com/news/world/corporations-are-turning-forest-credits-race-go-carbon-neutral-advocat-rcna7259> [accessed 18 December 2022].

23 For a perspective on the Anthropocene that arises from a critique of capitalism, see *Anthropocene or Capitalocene?: Nature, History, and the Crisis of Capitalism*, ed. by Jason W. Moore (Oakland, CA: PM Press, 2016).

This perspective recognizes the temporal and geographical intersections that need to be accounted for in order to review how categories like 'modern' and 'indigenous' have been pitched against each other by post-Enlightenment histories.[24]

One of the concepts that Rivera Cusicanqui offers for rethinking not only the historical complexities of coloniality but also how we imagine and build communities is the Aymara term *ch'ixi*. *Ch'ixi* refers to the colour grey, which, when observed from a close distance, reveals the black and white points that make up its texture. It is used to describe fluid beings, like the snake, who travel across borders and connect different worlds, like those of land and water. *Ch'ixi* beings embody multiple identities; they are neither male nor female, neither human nor nonhuman, and they flow like the serpent, which is also water.[25] The notion of *ch'ixi* designates interdependent worlds; on the one hand, it allows us to understand relationships of coloniality across boundaries, including those between north and south, while, on the other hand, it creates possibilities of commoning that elude the logic of duality. 'Perhaps', she writes, 'it will be possible to weave a ch'ixi epistemology of planetary value that will enable us to fulfill our common duties as human beings', while 'becom[ing] even more rooted in our own local communities, territories, and bioregions'.[26]

Building *ch'ixi* alliances means adopting the logic of impurity, through which human and nonhuman communities are recognized in their fundamental interconnectedness rather than divided by exclusionary categories. Thus,

---

24   Coletta, 'A World without Objects'.
25   Ibid.
26   *Ch'ixinakax utxiwa: On Practices and Discourses of Decolonization*, trans. Molly Geidel (Cambridge: Polity Press, 2010), p. 81.

this perspective also enables us to switch into an ecological epistemic mode where both individual and collective entities can be understood as participating in multiple worlds. In this respect, these theorizations are by no means abstract, but rather are attentive to material processes that are imbricated in the dialectical nature of oppression and resistance. The Nordic and Germanic etymology of 'entangle' refers back to 'seaweed', which ensnares wood, fish, and nets. In the same way, we are trapped in complex sets of relations whose contaminations can be revealed more fully through an entangled ecology perspective. 'Not being able to be in the middle', suggests Timothy Morton, 'is a big problem for ecological thinking. [...] [I]t edits out something vital to our experience of ecology, [...] the hesitation quality, feelings of unreality [...], feelings of the uncanny: feeling *weird*.'[27] A sense of possibility lies in the interstices that break dichotomic narratives of identity and follow the migratory routes of workers, plastics, foods, technologies, and ideas.

TOWARDS NON-ANTHROPOCENTRIC ALLIANCES

In approaching the category of the global south from the perspective of the history of knowledge, I hope that this brief reflection has offered a small contribution towards contaminating boundaries while recognizing the timely and necessary work done by global south scholarship. In his influential book on the history of knowledge, Peter Burke asks an important question: How do we determine what and who contributes to knowledge besides what falls

---

27   Timothy Morton, *All Art is Ecological* (London: Penguin Books, 2021), p. 2.

within western 'science'?[28] From this perspective, Menon's point about localism helps to assign political value to knowledges produced in any location, irrespective of claims to universality. I seem to steer back towards my initial question: '[W]ho is and who isn't deemed capable of knowing?'[29] This question can be expanded in a number of ways. For instance, one version may go like this: What kind of knowledge production is considered to be a viable tool for political decisions? This is where the global south as a framework is crucial in contributing not only to reshaping the debate about what constitutes knowledge but also to reviewing both the agents and the methods through which knowledge is produced.

However, as I have tried to suggest in the previous few pages, deeper lines are running across north and south, and I can trace these lines in my own professional and intellectual crossings, even if only anecdotally. The urgency to avoid abstract universalisms makes it relevant to challenge new forms of separation, which may otherwise continue to hinder the possibility of promoting critical alliances. Tracing the history of socio-ecological knowledge, as I have suggested, requires a conception of these relationships as impure, contaminated, and deeply entangled across those boundaries that continue to be anthropocentric and capitalocentric. Raising questions specifically about southern globality illuminates the political and economic hierarchies at play in any attempt at categorizing. At the same time, it is an opportunity to enrich existing epistemic frameworks for imagining new ways of making communities. For

---

28   Peter Burke, *What is the History of Knowledge?* (Oxford: Polity Press, 2015), p. 7.

29   Lukas M. Verburgt, 'The History of Knowledge and the Future History of Ignorance', *KNOW: A Journal on the Formation of Knowledge*, 4.1 (2020), p. 5 <https://doi.org/10.1086/708341>.

example, posthumanist philosophy struggles to find a way out of speciesism, and it largely continues to conceptualize the human as distinct from the animal. A *ch'ixi* worldview breaks this pattern by avoiding duality altogether. Similarly, disrupting the exclusionary dualism between indigeneity and modernity gives way to a shared sense of response-ability towards the unfolding of a planetary catastrophe. Building a non-anthropocentric future that responds to planetary threats requires planetary alliances.

Decolonialities and the Exilic Consciousness
Thinking from the Global South
MAHMOUD AL-ZAYED

THINKING ABOUT DECOLONIALITIES

Decoloniality presupposes the endurability of the coloniality of power that structures and controls various domains of life.[1] However, I want to use the term in the plural, *decolonialities*, to gesture towards both the multi-sited, normative formations of coloniality and the various ways in

*   In gratitude, I wish to thank Özgün Eylül İşcen, Iracema Dulley, and Christoph F. E. Holzhey for their comments and suggestions on this short chapter. All shortcomings, needless to say, remain my responsibility alone.

1   Aníbal Quijano, 'Coloniality and Modernity/Rationality', *Cultural Studies*, 21.2-3 (2007), pp. 168-78 <https://doi.org/10.1080/09502380601164353>; Aníbal Quijano, 'Coloniality of Power and Eurocentrism in Latin America', *International Sociology*, 15.2 (2000), pp. 215-32 <https://doi.org/10.1177/0268580900015002005>; Walter D. Mignolo, 'Introduction: Coloniality of Power and de-Colonial Thinking', *Cultural Studies*, 21.2-3 (2007), pp. 155-67 <https://doi.org/10.1080/09502380601162498>; Enrique D. Dussel,

which decolonization has been undertaken from different epistemic loci of enunciation to counter such colonial
matrices. These modes of decolonization attempt to create the means (theoretical or otherwise) to contest the
epistemic authority as well as the political economic structures underlying them within the history of the world capitalist system. In this respect, situating decolonial thought
within its location, its 'problem-space', links it with practice, its ultimate task of liberation.[2] Only in this way can
one expose the unmarked universalist tendencies that may
appear even within decolonial thought itself, avoiding the
problem of reproducing colonial relations of domination
and flattening its plurality and diverse trajectories. Therefore, the term I deploy here, decolonialities, refers to a
multitude of ongoing projects that aim at displacing hegemonic forms of colonial knowledge perpetuated by the
colonial matrix of power. However, they do not stop there:
they call for thinking from a different standpoint, engaging
multiple epistemological paradigms without assuming self-
sufficiency of thought, and thus, embracing a pluriversal
method of thinking.

If the overarching story of the world's historical formation reproducing 'monohumanism' has been undergirded

---

'Europe, Modernity, and Eurocentrism', trans. by Javier Krauel and
Virginia C. Tuma, *Nepantla: Views from South*, 1.3 (2000), pp. 465–78;
Walter D. Mignolo, *The Darker Side of Western Modernity: Global
Futures, Decolonial Options*, Latin America Otherwise: Languages,
Empires, Nations (Durham, NC: Duke University Press, 2011); Rita
Laura Segato, *The Critique of Coloniality: Eight Essays*, trans. Ramsey
McGlazer (New York: Routledge, 2022).

2   David Scott, *Conscripts of Modernity: The Tragedy of Colonial Enlightenment* (Durham, NC: Duke University Press, 2004). Scott argues for
making explicit the implicit set of questions and answers that shape
anticolonial arguments. For him, a problem-space is 'an ensemble of
questions and answers around which a horizon of identifiable stakes
(conceptual as well as ideological-political stakes) hangs' (p. 4).

by colonialism and racism,[3] then (counter)storytelling itself becomes a form of critique. Indeed, many decolonial
thinkers have pointed out the need to build up narratives
that interrogate various modes of coloniality and generate
perspectives and imaginaries beyond those colonial narratives. Along with postcolonial thinkers, they invite us to
displace the 'abstract universalism' of colonial narratives
that produce hierarchies of peoples, cultures, languages,
and knowledges. For instance, it was through 'race' and
'gender' as constituting categories that Eurocentric social
classifications of the world population were produced and
reproduced.[4] As an alternative to this colonial narrative
that simultaneously justifies and obscures the coloniality of
power, there arises an invitation to work with other imaginaries that are conceived as a network of multiple local histories that are violently negated, silenced, or repressed by the
machinery of colonialism/colonial (hi)story writing.[5] This
is also pitted against a relentless form of Eurocentrism —
understood here as the latent, false claim of self-sufficiency
by European thought — that manifests itself through the
perpetual negligence of other traditions of knowledge.[6]

---

3   See Sylvia Wynter, 'Unsettling the Coloniality of Being/Power/Truth/
     Freedom: Towards the Human, After Man, its Overrepresentation
     — An Argument', *CR: The New Centennial Review*, 3.3 (2003),
     pp. 257–337 <https://doi.org/10.1353/ncr.2004.0015>. Monohu-
     manism here refers to Wynter's conceptualization of the genealogy of
     the ethnocentric concept of Man. With its racial and colonial configur-
     ations within European history, it has been taken as the model of being
     human against which other humans are valued or devalued.

4   Quijano, 'Coloniality and Modernity/Rationality'; María Lugones,
     'Heterosexualism and the Colonial/Modern Gender System', *Hypatia*,
     22.1 (2007), pp. 186–209.

5   Walter D. Mignolo, *Local Histories/Global Designs: Coloniality, Sub-
     altern Knowledges, and Border Thinking*, Princeton Studies in Cul-
     ture/Power/History (Princeton, NJ: Princeton University Press, 2012).

6   Syed Farid Alatas, 'Religion and Concept Formation: Transcending
     Eurocentrism', in *Eurocentrism at the Margins*, ed. by Lutfi Sunar (New
     York: Routledge, 2016), pp. 87–102 (p. 98).

Thus, to think decolonially is to think against coloniality/colonialism by taking seriously the intellectual traditions, or traditions of intellection, of postcolonial spaces as loci of enunciation, emancipation, and generation of new forms of liberating knowledge. Here, I emphasize the possibilities of liberating knowledge because the act of decolonization is not *ipso facto* a liberating one; the claim of decolonization can be appropriated to reproduce and perpetuate colonial relations. The key idea here, however, is relationality. Coloniality is a form of relation that can take various forms and manifests itself in different locations and domains of life. Decolonialitites, in my view, could be thought of as a plasma that animates modes of thinking and being in the world that contribute to liberation. It does not claim the monopoly of ways toward liberation. Catherine Walsh, for instance, thinks that:

> [d]ecoloniality denotes ways of thinking, knowing, being, and doing that began with, but also precede, the colonial enterprise and invasion. It implies the recognition and undoing of the hierarchical structures of race, gender, heteropatriarchy, and class that continue to control life, knowledge, spirituality, and thought, structures that are clearly intertwined with and constitutive of global capitalism and Western modernity. Moreover, it is indicative of the ongoing nature of struggles, constructions, and creations that continue to work within coloniality's margins and fissures to affirm that which coloniality has attempted to negate.[7]

---

7   Catherine E. Walsh, 'The Decolonial For: Resurgences, Shifts, and Movements', in *On Decoloniality: Concepts, Analytics, Praxis*, ed. by Walter D. Mignolo and Catherine E. Walsh (Durham, NC: Duke University Press, 2018), pp. 15–32 (p. 17).

From this perspective, decoloniality does not yield a dogmatic belief or a form of fundamentalism.[8] Rather, it is a
call for opening a horizon in which no particular epistemological notion acts as a primary determinant that fixes the
social and institutional norms shaping knowledge production in a given location. Walsh continues:

> Decoloniality, in this sense, is not a static con-
> dition, an individual attribute, or a lineal point
> of arrival or enlightenment. Instead, decoloniality
> seeks to make visible, open up, and advance rad-
> ically distinct perspectives and positionalities that
> displace Western rationality as the only frame-
> work and possibility of existence, analysis, and
> thought.[9]

I agree with this formulation as long as one does not think
that displacing Western rationality and epistemology is the
prime and only task of decolonial thought in all locations of
critique. While this task is imperative in one location, it can
be paralysing in another. To insist again on thinking with
the 'problem-space' of decolonial thought, one can refer to
Malek Bennabi who, from his location, points out that colonialism can be a reality, a repressive and 'immense sabotage
of history', but also a myth, and an alibi, for not undertaking
the responsibility of liberation in domains in which colonialism cannot be incriminated.[10] Frantz Fanon, on the
other hand, rightly points out that the defensive position
of colonized intellectuals and their incessant and vehement

---

8   Fundamentalism is understood here as Ngũgĩ wa Thiong'o speaks of it:
    'Fundamentalism — economic, political or religious — is, essentially,
    an insistence that there is only one way of organizing reality.' Ngũgĩ wa
    Thiong'o, *Secure the Base: Making Africa Visible in the Globe*, The Africa
    List (London: Seagull Books, 2016), p. 23.

9   Walsh, 'The Decolonial For', p. 17.

10 Malek Bennabi, *Islam in History and Society*, trans. by Ashma Rashid
    (New Dehli: Kitabbhavan, 1999), pp. 47–48 and 57.

denunciations of colonialism 'reassure' the colonizer, who 'likened these scathing denunciations, outpourings of misery, and heated words to *an act of catharsis*'. For Fanon, '[e]ncouraging these acts would, in a certain way, avoid dramatization and clear the atmosphere.'[11] As for colonial regimes, one can always speak about colonialism as long as colonial structures are kept intact.

THINKING ABOUT EXILE AS A PLURILINGUAL LOCUS OF ENUNCIATION

After mapping the complicated and multi-layered experience of being displaced and exiled, Edward Said speaks of exile not as 'a privilege, but as an alternative to the mass institutions that dominate modern life' and invites the intellectuals living in exile to 'cultivate a scrupulous (not indulgent or sulky) subjectivity'.[12] When Theodor Adorno declared that it is the moral duty of the intellectual not to feel at home, he was alluding to the possibility of enacting the exilic consciousness within the home turf and suggesting that this option is an ethical one: 'It is part of morality not to be at home in one's home.'[13] Aligning with Adorno's refusal of institutionalized structures of knowledge-making, Said thought of cultivating an exilic detachment from 'homes' to see them with critical eyes. While the exile develops a sense of uneasiness with the whole concept of place and belonging in its conventional

---

11   Frantz Fanon, *The Wretched of the Earth*, trans. by Richard Philcox (New York: Grove Press, 2004), p. 173; emphasis added.

12   Edward W. Said, *Reflections on Exile and Other Essays* (Cambridge, MA: Harvard University Press, 2002), p. 184; emphasis added.

13   Theodor W. Adorno, *Minima Moralia: Reflections on a Damaged Life*, trans. by E. F. N. Jephcott, Radical Thinkers (London: Verso, 2005), p. 39.

or nationalistic terms, they sense their existence as being, as Said pinpoints, 'out of place':

> For an exile, habits of life, expression, or activity in the new environment inevitably occur against the memory of these things in another environment. Thus, both the new and the old environments are vivid, actual, occurring together contrapuntally. There is a unique pleasure in this sort of apprehension, especially if the exile is conscious of other contrapuntal juxtapositions that diminish orthodox judgment and elevate appreciative sympathy. There is also a particular sense of achievement in acting as if one were at home wherever one happens to be.[14]

There is a sense of territoriality in the notion of exile under which the idea of home lingers. In exile or any space of dislocation, one lives in a place that one can hardly lay claim to. One lives in a place marked with a constant force of nonbelonging, and usually occupies a position subaltern to the dominant culture that often constitutes the exile-displaced as an outsider. Thus, inhabiting the space of exile, one enters into a set of narratives and relations through which the dominant culture imposes its own ways of being and knowing. Ultimately, the mode of feeling-at-home is replaced by the sense of home-in-motion that one needs to construct to keep on living.

For those living within an exilic condition, there is a kind of double estrangement experienced as a result of displacement from 'home' and nonbelonging to hegemonic culture in the space of exile, as well as of the structural imposition of categories of knowledge that are either alien to one's experience or loaded with colonial and racialized presumptions. In a system that commits 'epistemicide'

---

14   Said, *Reflections on Exile*, p. 186.

by systematically oppressing particular ways of knowing while persistently interpellating the exilic subject as an outsider,[15] there is a latent demand for assimilation — or, to use its politically correct equivalent, integration — into the dominant system of being and knowing.

Hence, one always inhabits a paradoxical position anchored in the geographical enigma of one's location-in-motion, living in a perpetual crisis that invites one to see the world from the prism of exilic consciousness cultivated on the move. Said highlights the productive dimension of this exilic consciousness: 'Most people are principally aware of one culture, one setting, one home; exiles are aware of at least two, and this plurality of vision gives rise to an awareness of simultaneous dimensions, an awareness that — to borrow a phrase from music — is *contrapuntal*.'[16] The word contrapuntal here entails the possibility of reading and understanding beyond the monolingual and monoperspectival positioning, thereby enacting dialogical encounters involving multiple languages and perspectives without imposing any hierarchical structure. As Said embraces the term's musical reference, the idea of contrapuntal puts forth an imaginary in which different forms of knowledge reside together, with harmony and tension.

The reconfiguration of exile as a locus of enunciation recognizes that we are living in a pluriversal and multilingual world, since all those living in exile are cognizant of 'other(ed)' philosophies and knowledge productions. Exile as a condition enables one to generate knowledge from a space marked with plurality, even when one registers one's epistemic location. In other words, to inhabit

---

15   Boaventura de Sousa Santos, *Epistemologies of the South: Justice against Epistemicide* (New York: Routledge, 2014).

16   Said, *Reflections on Exile*, p. 186.

exile is to be able to think from the space across languages, a generative space, that facilitates the possibility of theorizing through a constant dialogue between one's language(s)/cultures and those of others. This generative space is a space of translation that is marked by a relational and processual nature as it animates 'plural thought that does not reduce the others (societies and individuals alike) to the sphere of its self-sufficiency'.[17] In this sense, exilic consciousness unsettles colonial relations between people, cultures, and languages.

In my reading, translation marked with self-insufficiency is something that resembles what Ngũgĩ wa Thiong'o calls the language of languages.[18] Only when marked with self-insufficiency can the act of translation potentially bring two languages into a generative space of meaning-making in ways that neither devalue nor annihilate each other's epistemic and symbolic systems. Ideally, this encounter becomes transformative, as no one dominates and, thus, limits the possibilities of meaning-making. Though translation transplants the translated text onto a different 'lingual [and oral] memory',[19] it does not necessarily reduce the translated text to the target language's vision of theorizing and meaning-making or

---

17 Abdelkebir Khatibi, *Plural Maghreb: Writings on Postcolonialism*, trans. by P. Burcu Yalim, Suspensions: Contemporary Middle Eastern and Islamicate Thought (London: Bloomsbury Academic, 2019), p. 6.

18 Ngũgĩ wa Thiong'o, *Globalectics: Theory and the Politics of Knowing*, The Wellek Library Lectures in Critical Theory (New York: Columbia University Press, 2012), p. 61.

19 Alton Becker, *Beyond Translation: Essays toward a Modern Philology* (Ann Arbor: University of Michigan Press, 1995). 'Lingual memory' constitutes the repertoire of what Becker sometimes calls 'prior texts', oral or textual, as well as 'words and silences that shape a context, in space, in time, in social relations, in nature, and in emotions and subtle intimations' (p. 12). It is that which makes the languaging of language and its meanings familiar.

rigidly fix this text within the host language's system of references. Thus, meaning-making can remain multilingual and multidimensional.

Indeed, reducing the linguistic world through which one theorizes to that of the other is a form of reduction that often takes the shape of colonial imposition due to the power asymmetries constitutive of the rhetoric of multi-lingualism in the European setting. The exilic subject, or any alert bilingual reader for that matter, avoids this form of reductionism precisely because of the awareness that languages coming into contact — though differentially — have the potential to activate the unsettling play of a lingual/oral double memory. In this way, those who confront an exilic condition or displacement can avoid the tyranny of monolingualism and the self-sufficiency of thought. Even though this quality of thinking is gained through an existentially painful experience, it does not be-long merely to those who live in multilingual worlds of exile and displacement at large. As Said and Adorno point out, it is even desirable to cultivate an exilic consciousness in order to free the act of thinking from its own limits, whether historical or structural.

Still, the experience of living in exile or any form of displacement can be existentially shattering for those going through it, and there is nothing to romanticize about it. One must always think of refugees, the displaced, the dis-possessed, and the unimaginable numbers of dead people en route who were buried in land or water. What under-girds the tendencies of romanticizing is the unwillingness to mud one's feet in the slums of the political. In this respect, it is critical to reflect on how one's positional-ity involves class, gender, and race-related configurations. Therefore, it is significant to remember that we live in an age of mass displacement and migration due to the presence of oppressive, genocidal state regimes and imperial wars with unequally distributed global impacts.

EXILE AND DECOLONIALITIES: THINKING FROM THE GLOBAL SOUTH

Theorizing from and through the Global South entails registering the location of intellection.[20] Dilip Menon thinks of the category of Global South 'as a project, a conceptual and experiential category that is not a mere geographical agglomeration',[21] and extends it into an invitation to 'rethink the world anew *from a different standpoint*'.[22] Yet whether one thinks of the Global South as a metaphor, an epistemic choice, or even as a geopolitical or experiential category, the weight of geography looms large due to the presence of heterogeneities that constitute it.[23] Thus, the task of relocating the act of theorization derives from the fact that each geographical location generates its set of problems and questions, and decolonial critics respond to the latter while eventually orienting themselves to the planetary consciousness at large.

However, in the situation of the displaced, the attempt to register one's epistemic location becomes a more com-

---

20   See Walter D. Mignolo, 'Epistemic Disobedience, Independent Thought and Decolonial Freedom', *Theory, Culture & Society*, 26.7–8 (2009), pp. 159–81 <https://doi.org/10.1177/0263276409349275>; *Changing Theory: Concepts from the Global South*, ed. by Dilip M. Menon (Milton Park: Routledge, 2022); Dilip M. Menon, 'Thinking about the Global South', in *The Global South and Literature*, ed. by Russell West-Pavlov (Cambridge: Cambridge University Press, 2018), pp. 34–44 <https://doi.org/10.1017/9781108231930.003>.

21   Menon, 'Thinking about the Global South', p. 36.

22   Ibid., p. 34.

23   Menon rightly warns against the tendencies to reduce the South to 'a *merely* theoretical space, leading us to verbal prestidigitation like North of the South, South of the North, and so on — Detroit as South in the United States, Johannesburg as North in Africa' (Menon, *Changing Theory*, p. 3).

plicated task: One needs to attend to the set of problems and questions in one's immediate (new) environment as well as to the sets generated elsewhere. These two sets of questions and priorities may intersect, especially given the planetary scale of the urgent issues we face today. Nonetheless, the enigmatic problem of the exilic condition comes forth in intellectual settings that deny the plurilingual and collective nature of thinking. These settings also often involve implicit or explicit forms of racism/monohumanism supplemented by exclusionary narratives constituting the dominance of nation state and citizenship paradigms. Thus, such knowledge ecosystems devalue and dismiss a knowing subject that speaks from a different epistemic standpoint. In opposition, the figure that insists on thinking otherwise cultivates a decolonial attitude, which entails incessant border crossing, negotiation, and translation.

Reflecting on these conditions of theorization which constitute my location, I wonder: Does exilic consciousness necessarily promote decolonial thinking, or, more specifically, what is it to theorize from the Global South while one is displaced in the Global North? One interesting formulation that brings decolonial thinking close to exile comes from Walter Mignolo, who somehow echoes Said's contrapuntal method. After citing Paul Gilroy's *Black Atlantic*, which marks the beginning of the end of the land-centric political imagination of location, Mignolo offers a connection between exile and border thinking:

> Now, if exiles (as well as diasporic people, immigrants, and refugees) are all a form of 'location-in-movement' rather than 'location-in-land' (and both in-movement and in-land are understood as 'places'), we could perhaps argue that border thinking is a necessary consequence of these sorts of locations. Exiles 'have' to leave the territory

> where they belonged and, consequently, are lo-
> cated in a particular kind of subaltern position,
> and that subaltern position creates the conditions
> for double consciousness and border thinking. To
> be in exile is to be simultaneously in two loca-
> tions and in a subaltern position. And those are
> the basic conditions for border thinking to emerge
> at different levels: epistemic, political and ethic.[24]

Enacting the plurality of thought and taking an exilic point
of view, theorizing from the Global South entails ushering
in perspectives and knowledges that challenge the coloni-
ally administrated world. This, in effect, implies engaging
with a spectrum of intellectual traditions that have been
part of the Global South. Yet, they have not been thought
of as a body of knowledge production with distinct homo-
logical affinities, capable of offering perspectives that challenge formulations perpetuated by colonial epistemologies
that assume various forms of monolingualism and monohumanism. This is an intellectual chance to generate and
think with imaginaries capable of unsettling the capitalist
and war-oriented world, imagining a more just and better future. Exilic consciousness is potentially decolonial as
long as it existentially enacts the struggle against colonial-
ities in order to undo them. It is decolonial in as much as
it facilitates the cultivation of habits of thinking that challenge hegemonic forms of knowledge, hence imagining the
planet differently in order to undo the perpetual silences
and the erasures of different ways of knowing, sensing, and
doing that are devalued or annihilated by the dominant
local cultures universalized by the coloniality of power.

---

24   L. Elena Delgado and Rolando J. Romero, 'Local Histories and Global
     Designs: An Interview with Walter Mignolo', *Discourse*, 22.3 (2000),
     pp. 7–33 (p. 15) <https://doi.org/10.1353/dis.2000.0004>.

Berlin's Killjoys
Feminist Art from the Global South
ŞİRİN FULYA ERENSOY

INTRODUCTION

On 24 September 2022, the Women* Life Freedom Collective,[1] based in Berlin, called for a protest against the Islamic Regime of Iran to show solidarity with the protesters of Iran. This new wave of protests in Iran began in reaction to Zhina Mahsa Amini's death following injuries suffered in police custody. Zhina Mahsa was a twenty-two-year-old Kurdish-Iranian woman who was stopped by the morality police because she was not wearing her hijab in accordance with the country's laws on Islamic dress code. She was taken into police custody and died in the hospital three days later. Although the coroner's report states that Zhina Mahsa died of a heart attack, her family denies she

---

1   Please refer to their Instagram page: <https://www.instagram.com/womanlifefreedomcollective/> [accessed 30 September 2022].

had heart problems, insisting that she died of skull injuries caused by blows to her head.[2]

During the protest held in Wedding's Nettelbeckplatz, performance artist Shahrzad Sdred ripped off her hijab, decrying the system that forced her to cover her body. She then ensued with her performance, removing each item of clothing one by one. Sdred cried out to the crowd: 'I had to cover my body there because I was a woman. But I have to cover my body here too, because it is not white enough. I reject your standards!' Discussions on Zhina Mahsa in the German media prompted a reaction from another Berlin-based Iranian artist, Rosh Zeeba, who commented on the coverage by stating in an Instagram story: 'Can we talk about Iran without Islamophobia? Why ask Alice Schwarzer her opinion instead of having a more intersectional approach? Imagine practicing feminism from a non-western point of view....'[3]

As I recently discovered, Alice Schwarzer, whom Zeeba refers to, is a German journalist and prominent feminist. Yet, one wonders: what if German media had reached out to other journalists from the Iranian diaspora already residing in Berlin, the exile capital of Europe? In this respect, Zeeba's reaction speaks to many feminists from the Global South, who have been criticizing white feminism for being depoliticized in that there is a gap between the values they claim to hold and their willingness to do the work needed to connect thought and action. Indeed, Feminista Berlin, during one of their rallies, called

---

2   Reuters, 'Events in Iran since Mahsa Amini's Arrest and Death in Custody', *Reuters*, 12 December 2022 <https://www.reuters.com/world/middle-east/events-iran-since-mahsa-aminis-arrest-death-custody-2022-10-05/> [accessed 6 February 2023].

3   The Instagram page of Rosh Zeeba is: <instagram.com/rosh_zeeba/> [accessed 6 October 2023].

on the German minister of foreign affairs, Annalena Baerbock, to implement the feminist foreign policy she claimed she would foster when she was appointed.[4]

This call joined a growing trend in which it is demanded that Global North governments adopt feminist foreign policies to critically address structural power imbalances and find more sustainable solutions with more inclusive decision-making processes.

However, the urgent condition of the current situation in Iran demands immediate action rather than waiting for such slow-moving policy changes. Iranian diaspora groups argue the actions of Germany and the EU so far have had no real consequences for Iran, as executions are accelerating, persecution and military attacks on marginalized groups continue, and the arbitrary arrest of protestors is ever-growing. They state that the symbolic actions taken by Germany absolve it from responsibility while undermining democratic forces in Iran, thereby exemplifying a gesture of critical complicity (on the side of Germany). It was only in January 2023, three months after the protests began and following the fourth execution, that Germany decided to summon its Iranian ambassador. Thus, there is a long way to go before the so-called feminist foreign policy is applied to its full effect.

UNPACKING UNDERSTANDINGS OF HOME

The plight of Iranian artists refers to a reality beyond the context of these recent protests. They relay the experience of a duality related to the limits set on their so-called freedoms in the West — limits that essentially remind them of their otherness, as expressed by Sdred and Zeeba. My

---

4   Please refer to their Instagram page: <https://www.instagram.com/feminista.berlin/> [accessed 12 December 2022].

observations and interactions as an embedded researcher in feminist activist circles of Berlin have shown me that women* activists in exile often have the ability to move beyond the boundaries of the given culture and question them. These women* activists in exile recognize the cultural constructedness of the given cultural boundaries because they are explicitly positioned at the margins of this constructedness and thus experience how mechanisms of inclusion and exclusion operate and impact their day-to-day life.

For example, Özlem Sarıyıldız's aptly titled video *Welcomed to Germany?* (Figure 1) asks its protagonists to reflect directly on these mechanisms.[5] Özlem is an activist and artist from Turkey who has been living in Berlin since 2017. In the mentioned video work, she asks a variety of new-wave migrants from Turkey about their experience in Germany. Queer musician Gizem Oruç's answer, 'Being a migrant is a full-time activism', summarizes the lived experience of the constant struggle for belonging in Germany.[6] *Welcomed to Germany?* and its spotlight on peripheral subjectivities in this new space of living have led me to think about the notion of home.

Feminists have long challenged socially imposed understandings of the home: starting in the 1970s, feminists actively rejected the so-called private haven of the home, which was defined as secure, safe, and stable. They brought to light the lived realities that haunted those confined within four walls. By revealing the dynamics of gender domination at work in the home, which limited the role of women* to domestic and reproductive labour, feminist approaches have shattered

---

5   *Welcomed to Germany?*, dir. by Özlem Sarıyıldız (Utopictures, 2018).
6   Ibid.

Figure 1. Özlem Sarıyıldız, *Welcomed to Germany?*, 2018,
screenshot from video. Image credit: Özlem Sarıyıldız,
utopictures.com.

the supposed wholesomeness of the home and the
concurrent expectations implicit within it. Indeed, home
entailed a place where women* served men, a place of
captivity for the sake of the nourishment and care of men,
who, on the contrary, had ultimate authority within the
household yet limited responsibility for the domestic
and child-rearing duties that take place within it. It was
revealed that, during the pandemic, the home became a
domestic prison for many women*, who were abused and
violated, and as a result felt homeless at home.

Drawing from my personal and professional experiences, home becomes an impossibility for subjects forcibly
displaced from their point of origin and yet who are not
welcomed in their new environments. Nation states have

become increasingly concerned with the notion of home in reaction to the accelerated waves of migration. The need to assimilate the figure of the migrant in order to protect the identity of the nation state has unveiled discriminatory practices within restrictive migration policies. In turn, these policies have become the defining feature of what constitutes home for millions in transit, creating permanent states of transience.

Thus, as supported by empirical evidence from my research subjects, while many leave home to escape oppressive politics and deeply entrenched gender norms, as well as to gain economic independence and political freedom, they are met with further pressures in their new living environments. This sense of temporality is accentuated further by the ways in which these adopted homes try to discipline the migrant: the constant state of being surveilled and the need to complete administrative processes that, far from welcoming, impose the notion that one could be expelled at the slightest wrong turn. Having to narrate convincing stories of victimhood creates a vicious cycle that prolongs and postpones the process of belonging.

While Berlin has irrevocably changed as a result of becoming a strategic and political locus of migration and exile in recent years, many feel that it only accepts those who do not push the boundaries of the discursive comfort zones of German society. While this has allowed some people a fresh start, it has not arrived without its challenges. Newcomers in Berlin navigate the menace of daily racism, rising right-wing politics, and the housing crisis — which is itself accentuated by racism. They fight daily to construct an alternative narrative and future, searching for safe spaces where they can critically and emotionally engage their new present reality. This process of homing, as conceptualized by Paolo Boccagni, entails an 'existential struggle towards a good-enough state of being at home', thereby highlighting the processual constitution of home.[7]

BUILDING NEW HOMES: FEMINIST APPROACHES

As a researcher focusing on audiovisual production by activists in exile, I have been conducting semi-structured, in-depth interviews with video activists from Turkey.[8] In the meantime, I found myself contemplating the concept of home, as I was also living between two localities. Even though my main interest in the project was reflecting on how the experience of exile had impacted their activism, one of the interview questions I asked all participants was about their understanding of what home is, and their approach to homing. I explored how their feelings relating to belonging, inclusion, and acceptance changed over time; indeed, what I encountered was very much the sense that being-at-home was a 'shifting ideal and condition', 'an active, processual and potentially never-ending endeavour'.[9]

I was also particularly interested in this question because my fieldwork in 2021 overlapped with the sixtieth year of migration from Turkey to Germany since the first German-Turkish Recruitment Agreement in 1961. There have been extensive studies on the Agreement's long-term impacts on so-called guest workers (*Gastarbeiter*innen*) who immigrated from Turkey. Their social realities were marked by the dual nature of transience and integration: searching for economic prosperity and personal freedoms

---

7   Paolo Boccagni, 'Homing: A Category for Research on Space Appropriation and "Home-Oriented" Mobilities', *Mobilities*, 17.4 (2022), pp. 585–601 (p. 585) <https://doi.org/10.1080/17450101.2022.2046977>.

8   For more information on this research project, please refer to the project website: <https://www.videoact.eu/> [accessed 10 May 2023].

9   Boccagni, 'Homing', pp. 586 and 591.

and yet faced low wages, strenuous working conditions, and the general lack of hospitality coming from the host country.[10] Their problems were not considered to be the problems of the greater German society, but those of temporary guests, who were expected to leave at the end of their two-year contracts. As a result, while cultural segregation was part of the exclusionary reactions of German society, it also became a strategy for migrants to combat official policies and create safe spaces in their new German contexts. This allowed guest workers to have some stability and orientation as they navigated the new political, cultural, and economic landscape they were inhabiting. However, women faced a dual displacement since they became prisoners within their own communities. Whether they were guest workers themselves or coming to Germany as brides, women occupied a space where they were marginalized, facing oppressive patriarchal traditions within the diaspora and being perceived as victims by the larger German society. As such, the voice of women became central to understanding the experience of home as plural, complex, and shifting, oscillating between the real and the imaginary.

The disruptive power that feminist approaches made way for directed me to explore another project in conjunction with my research. To better understand how the city transforms itself as a result of migration and how belonging within it is experienced, I joined the Women*

---

10   See studies that provide social and political analysis of the problems of social integration through the perspective of migrants, effectively questioning the prevailing notion of German tolerance and its implications for the integration process: Rob Burns, 'Images of Alterity: Second-Generation Turks in the Federal Republic', *The Modern Language Review*, 94.3 (1999), pp. 744–57 <https://doi.org/10.2307/3736999>; *Turkish Culture in German Society Today*, ed. by David Horrocks and Eva Kolinsky (New York: Berghahn, 1996).

Artists' Web Archive project (WAWA),[11] which was initiated by the Apartment Project.[12] WAWA presents an
online archive of women* artists based in Berlin. It aims at
the creation, indexing, and distribution of information on
Berlin-based women* artists from Afghanistan, Palestine,
Iran, Iraq, Syria, Turkey, and Yemen.

These countries have undergone severe conflicts and
wars in the past decades, leading to willing or forced migration. Many women* artists moved to Berlin's transnational
space to continue their creative professions. Such mobility
has reshaped the dynamic and diverse artistic landscape of
Berlin. Thus, WAWA's goal is to keep traces of this changing
scene and provide more visibility for new artists. Moreover,
when coming to Germany, women* artists coming from
these countries carry with them the experiences of othering they have faced as a result of cultural practices and traditions. This gender-based othering is then compounded
with race-based othering in Germany. In this regard, it felt
crucial to foster a sense of togetherness and community
where a collaborative environment can emerge out of these
encounters among artists.

As members of WAWA, we have been organizing face-
to-face meetings with other members to introduce the
archive and our initial ideas. We asked all members: 'What
kind of archive would you like to be part of?' This archive
is thus designed collectively and horizontally, facilitated
by the WAWA team, and hosted by the Apartment Project. The archive enables the participant to search through

11 Women* Artists' Web Archive, 2023 <https://wawa-network.org>
    [accessed 15 January 2023].
12 Apartment Project Berlin, 2023 <http://berlin.apartmentproject.org>
    [accessed 21 January 2023]. This space, established in the Neukölln
    neighbourhood of Berlin in 2012, primarily focuses on collaborative
    artistic practices with a focus on displacement, belonging, and (mi-
    grant) identities.

artists, geographies, themes, and disciplines. Each artist summarizes her/their creative practice with keywords that make up the section themes and presents herself/themself through the disciplinary and geographical categories to which she/they feels a sense of belonging. Moreover, the archive puts together a regular newsletter, providing information regarding the events and activities in which each member is involved, thereby multiplying our venues of togetherness. In essence, we strive to achieve visibility for women* artists by creating a network of care gestures and activating an embodied archive through online and offline spaces that facilitate discussion, collaboration, and sharing.

One of the ways in which we aim to activate this archive is through an exhibition. Titled *Beyond Home* and conceived with my colleagues Selda Asal and Özlem Sarıyıldız, the exhibition will bring together perspectives of migrant feminists that make visible the contradictory understanding evoked by the home and deconstruct the image of the home that has been historically imposed and perpetuated in patriarchal contexts. It aims to open up a space for homemaking experiences that break the monopoly on decisions about which belongings are accepted in a given culture and society. As such, our exhibition intends to dismantle the patriarchal discourses and practices concerning the home and allow those who are spoken for and silenced to speak back. By presenting the variety of approaches to the concept of home and its lived experience in Berlin's artistic and intellectual community, the exhibition will showcase the tensions embedded within the process of homing. In this way, it will shed light upon the workings of power that allow some notions of home and identity to be accepted and others to be violently relegated to the margins.

Hence, for our exhibition, we embraced the understanding that to 'render a new order of ideas perceptible', we need to 'disorder ideas'.[13] Our following realization was that this could be possible only if the violence of the patriarchal order and its institutions is exposed. Indeed, we are inspired by what Sara Ahmed has called a 'feminist killjoy', which is an individual who raises uncomfortable questions, necessary truths, and unpopular opinions and thus disturbs the conventional order of things so that transformation can ensue. Ahmed characterizes this movement as a shelter in and of itself because it allows for an understanding of

> how to live better in an unjust and unequal world [...] how to create relationships with others that are more equal; how to find ways to support those who are not supported or are less supported by social systems; how to keep coming up against histories that have become concrete, histories that have become as solid as walls.[14]

Our exhibition will showcase killjoy stories from multiple subject positions that go beyond romanticized clichés of the home, forced positionings of either here or there, and imaginative journeys that feed displacement discourses. In this manner, this exhibition aims to create new alliances through collective togetherness, questioning structures of power relentlessly, revealing them continuously, and engaging with them structurally. While this may cause us to 'bump into the world that does not live in accordance with the principles we try to live', it will be a vessel through which repressed experiences will come into the open, providing an opportunity to shift and impact understandings.[15]

---

13 Sara Ahmed, *Living a Feminist Life* (Durham, NC: Duke University Press, 2017), p. 251.

14 Ibid., p. 1.

15 Ibid., p. 255.

At the time of writing this piece, in early 2023, we plan the exhibition to take place in the summer of the same year at Kunstraum Kreuzberg/Bethanien. Significantly, this space is a public institution, part of the Friedrichshain-Kreuzberg District Council. Its funding comes from the Capital Cultural Fund, established by the German Federal Government and the State of Berlin. Using available public funding mechanisms allows underrepresented and intersectional experiences to carve out a space in the public arena. Otherwise, we often end up overlooking, if not flattening, substantive differences between the conditions and trajectories of particular movements across spatial borders, most often reducing their positions and demands to a rubric of European liberal ideals. What differs here and goes beyond the pigeonholing of migrant struggles is that these stories are disseminated without the controlling framework of European narratives; this is an approach that insists on combatting the persistent challenges with artistic equity. Feminism from the global south indeed has such a bottom-up approach: instead of waiting passively to be (mis)represented by its counterparts, it has taken the means of production into its own hands in order to decentralize claims to reality.

CONCLUSION

So, what becomes of this new home? What becomes of the city of Berlin in which we live and come together? Does the lack of a home create a common bond? Does one become a community with those who have this shared experience? Well, yes, and history shows us that too: many marginalized groups have showcased alternative forms of home-making, resisting the limitations within public spaces. They have undertaken collective homemaking practices that become embodied forms of resistance and affirmations of life. Queer practices of homemaking, for example, have become sites of construction and expression of queer identities when the heteronormative and fascist governance, which violently represses their bodies and voices, doesn't allow otherwise. Similarly, for BIPOC women*, despite all the vulnerabilities it entails, the home becomes a reprieve from the racism present in the public sphere. Consequently, these communities in Berlin are resisting the restrictive walls imposed upon them by drawing on collective solidarity, going beyond their safe spaces and voicing their demands in the public sphere.

Looking at the ongoing protests against the Islamic regime in Iran, we see each protest gaining momentum, with diverse crowds coming together. For three months, Feminista Berlin organized a protest in front of the headquarters of the Green Party, with sit-ins lasting twenty-four hours each day, condemning the passivity and critical complicity of German foreign policy towards Iran. In order to create a more just society, the protestors demanded that the officials uphold the values they preach; however, the protestors were not addressed by any representative of the Green Party.

Despite these political authorities ignoring such demands, Berlin is progressively becoming the biggest hub for Middle Eastern feminism. Feminists across Europe came to Berlin for the largest feminist march against the Islamic regime on 22 October 2022. Since then, the protests have grown into expanding solidarity through demonstrations, performances, readings, forums, and public interventions. These feminist killjoys will continue to occupy, create, and destabilize the imposed norms, rendering all uncomfortable until hypocritical structures are done away with in the name of human rights, equality, and freedom of speech.

Challenges of Southern Knowledge Production
Reflections on/through Iran

FIROOZEH FARVARDIN AND NADER TALEBI

INTRODUCTION: CHALLENGES OF SOUTHERN POSITIONALITY

While we were finishing the first draft of this chapter, a revolution was unfolding in Iran. It was not the first revolution in its history. However, like other parts of the Middle East, Iran has often been portrayed as an exception, a space of permanent conflicts and sectarian struggles, which reduces history to certain dichotomies such as modern-traditional and Islamist-secular. This reductive over-simplification renders the unfolding feminist revolution in Iran, with its slogan 'Women, Life, Freedom', rooted in the Kurdish struggle around the Middle East and, particularly, Rojava, more unthinkable. For it cannot account for the multiplicity of forces with diverse histories that are involved. Many of those who are active in this revolution are marginalized in the knowledge production on the country and in efforts to decolonize it. In other words, the new revolutionary subjects of the ongoing revolution are mainly those subjects and forces whose accounts and deeds are missing in knowledge productions about Iran.

We aim to elaborate and reflect on three intertwined challenges in our attempts to discuss the conditions of possibility for knowledge production on, in, and through the Global South. All these challenges are related to the politics of scale. How does a specific scale become dominant due to a particular history of power struggles? How does it contribute to the reproduction of certain power relations? Scale, in this sense, is socially (re)produced through individual and institutional actions. In other words, social practices can create and transform scales. Thus, the dominant scale results from historically accumulated power struggles that act as spatial organizers of actions. In the case of knowledge production, it is perhaps more evident in the scale of problematization, where specific scales are reproduced at the expense of others. Is this a 'local' issue or a 'regional' one? What is the scale of available data? One can think of the domination of methodological nationalism in this sense. Another way of tackling the politics of scale is by examining its impact on the political economy of publishing scholarly work: At what scale of framing does the issue at hand have a better chance of publication? Moreover, the politics of scale is also about evaluating its consequences in terms of knowledge production. Do we consider the outcomes of our knowledge production on a local scale or map it on a global one? What kinds of power relations are reproduced as crystallized in specific scales?

Considering the politics of scale and focusing on specific cases of knowledge production about Iran in recent years, we discuss the challenges and risks that we, as critical scholars, face in attempting to go beyond the dominant Northern perspectives.

First, the problematic of positionality: we, as scholars who claim that it is possible to theorize through the Global South(s), need to reflect on our positionality. This reflection should not be limited to intersectional social status regarding social class, ethnic/national, and gender/sexual relations; it should also include in-between positions in the academic realm, located between the margins of the North and, to some degree, the core of Southern perspectives. A kind of in-betweenness comes from occupying the marginal position of a migrant in Europe in contrast to the relatively more central position that one occupied on a smaller scale — consider the position of a Persian/Shi'a/male migrant in Europe and that of a Kurdish/Sunni/woman living in Iran. In other words, we are in the borderland and face its positive and negative effects on how we deal with theorizing in, from, and through the Global South(s).[1] In this respect, we need to acknowledge and reflect on the reality that the significant efforts of decolonization and our problematizations of cognitive Northern-Southern divisions have come from 'here', the Global North's zones of knowledge production, instead of 'there', i.e., the sites of struggles and knowledge production in the Global South(s).

Second, the hierarchization of sites and zones of knowledge production in both the Global North(s) and the Global South(s) assigns a higher degree of importance and visibility to one specific context, site, or geography of knowledge production. This mechanism conse-

---

1   Gloria Anzaldúa, *Borderlands/La Frontera: The New Mestiza* (San Francisco, CA: Aunt Lute Books, 2012).

quently naturalizes the Global North's false claims about 'cognitive superiority', while imposing the rationality of the Northern perspectives as the dominant mode of rationality within the Southern zones. This hierarchization underscores the continuation of cognitive colonialism, in which one adopts and internalizes the epistemic principles of Eurocentrism and so-called Northern rationalities.[2] Therefore, we should assert that not every attempt at decolonizing knowledge production has contributed to overcoming power imbalances. In other words, by endowing the Northern sites of knowledge production with a higher degree of importance and initiating our problematization from 'here', we neglect the negative consequences of our decolonizing efforts for the Global South(s).

Third, the institutionalization and centralization of knowledge production on and through the Global South(s) in area studies have historically caused the (trans)formation of area studies (such as Middle Eastern studies, Iranian studies, Latin American studies, etc.) into by-products of colonialism. Consequently, a particular power structure and in-between positionality have been imposed on those who work on and from the Global South(s), thus legitimizing hierarchization between sites and zones of knowledge production.

In order to elaborate on these challenges, which certainly have affected the conditions of possibility for producing knowledge on, in, and through the Global South(s), we discuss two examples concerning Iran in the following pages.

---

2   Boaventura de Sousa Santos, *Decolonising the University: The Challenge of Deep Cognitive Justice* (Newcastle upon Tyne: Cambridge Scholars Publishing, 2018).

NATIVISM IN IRAN

Attempts to decolonize and resist the global power structures often include searching for or returning to neglected capacities and so-called marginalized figures in the Global South(s). Discussing nativism is particularly important as we witness an increasing interest in Iranian nativist intellectuals, among whom there are scholars, mainly working within Global North academia, that we identify as holding in-between positions.[3] The Iranian nativist intellectual production mainly dates back to the 1960s and 1970s and has close ties to Islamists and the later official nativist discourses in the Islamic Republic. We, therefore, find it problematic that these nativist anti-Western or anti-colonial figures (e.g., Ali Shariati and Jalal Al-e-Ahmad) are frequently presented in the Global North as marginalized decolonial thinkers, regardless of the present power dynamics, particularly on (sub)national scales.

It is noteworthy that we do not talk about nativism per se but rather about the conditions of possibility for theorizing from and through Iran as part of the Global South(s), considering the dominance of nativism as the official discourse monopolizing the academic sphere in this country, particularly in the humanities,[4] which goes hand in hand with the more general philosophy of the Islamic Republic. In the following paragraphs, we briefly discuss the challenges and complexities of such efforts as well as the risk of reproducing colonial hierarchies and enforcing dominant repressive nativist discourses in Iran through

---

3   Afshin Matin-Asgari, *Both Eastern and Western: An Intellectual History of Iranian Modernity* (Cambridge: Cambridge University Press, 2018), pp. 190–222.

4   This pattern is also apparent in other fields, such as Islamic Economics, Islamic Medicine, and Islamic Physics.

them. After all, the road to hell is often paved with good intentions.

Even though the above-mentioned figures cannot merely be reduced to the perspective of the Islamic Republic, detaching them from their historical contexts, meaning their close ties with nativism, is also problematic. Historically, nativism in Iran has been a call to return to the self. Toward the mid-nineteenth century, the Persian Empire underwent several changes resulting from semi-colonial conditions,[5] integration into the world market, and the introduction of capitalism. In this sense, nativism grew from a collective disappointment in finding allies against colonial powers such as the British and Russian Empires on the international scene.

According to Negin Nabavi, the discourse of 'authentic culture' rose in Iran, during the 1960s and 1970s, in response to 'a combination of Third-Worldism and the movement of counterculture predominant in the West'.[6] This discourse also targeted the central part of the then dominant discourse on modernization, which has, from its beginning, advocated for a universal departure from what is formulated as the 'traditional'.

Modernization discourse, as a vital part of state-building projects, has been one of the two main trends of universalism that shaped the backbones of knowledge production in and on Iran. The other one is Soviet Marxism. Interestingly, both universalistic approaches share an understanding of history as linear, although with

---

5   Iran has never officially been a colony but became a site of semi-colonial intervention and competition, mainly by the British and Russian empires. Perhaps it was this very competition that saved it from becoming a colony of one particular colonizer.

6   Negin Nabavi, *Intellectuals and the State in Iran: Politics, Discourse, and the Dilemma of Authenticity* (Gainesville: University Press of Florida, 2003), p. 104.

different stations and destinations. Modernization theory and related concepts have constituted what is and remains the most influential social-theoretical approach in Iran. Indeed, they have shaped the main body of sociological studies as the 'sociology of development'.[7]

In this sense, nativism in Iran, by calling for a return to the 'self', has been a response to the claim of universality by modernization theory and Marxism. It means that progress will be achieved by reviving what we were before instead of imitating what is happening elsewhere. Before the revolution, the return was pointed towards a narrative of the pre-Islamic Persian Empire. However, instead of the archaic, pre-Islamic Aryan self that was prominent in the pre-revolutionary era, the post-revolutionary Islamic state has adopted a return to an 'Islamic self'. Interestingly but not to our surprise, perhaps, both narratives of this self are colonial, orientalist, and entangled with imperial aspects of Iran. After all, this self has been historically constructed in the context of power struggles across different scales.

The most celebrated Iranian anti-Western intellectuals, such as Ali Shariati and Jalal Al-e-Ahmad, appeared in this historical context. While they cannot be held responsible for the dominant Islamist discourse of the post-revolutionary era, one should not forget their contribution to what later served as justifications for what happened after the revolution that none of them lived to see. To name one of the post-revolutionary incidents relevant to knowledge production, we can mention the Cultural Revolution (1980–83) in Iran and its purge of so-called Western ideas, including but not limited to Marxism, in the name of Is-

---

7   Ebrahim Towfigh and Shirin Ahmadnia, 'How to Overcome "Oriental" Sociology?', in *Spatial Social Thought: Local Knowledge in Global Science Encounters*, ed. by Michael Kuhn (New York: Columbia University Press, 2014), pp. 313–26 (p. 318).

lamic and native identity, which was followed in the 1980s with mass execution of the opposition.

The purge was narrated as an effort to reform Iranian culture, which resonates with attempts to correct 'traditional' culture in the modernization discourse historically connected with colonialism. In both cases, the dominant argument was that there are problems in people's 'culture' that need to be addressed or reformed to make way for the further progress of society. Nevertheless, this concern with authentic culture, which was always rendered religiously after the revolution, was not limited to that purge. One can see that connected terminologies such as 'cultural invasion by the West' (تهاجم فرهنگی غرب), the 'soft war against Iran' (جنگ نرم علیه ایران), and 'Cultural NATO' (ناتوی فرهنگی) have become usual topics in crucial speeches by the supreme leader of Iran, Ali Khamenei[8] (and before him, Khomeini).[9] To Khamenei, the material war mutated

---

[8]   For example: 'Today there is a vast cultural invasion against Islam which is not directly linked to the revolution. This invasion is more extensive than only targeting the revolution: it targets Islam' (Khamenei, 28 November 1989); or 'The enemies focus on culture more than anything else' (Khamenei, 21 March 2014). These speeches are compiled in 'Cultural Invasion on Islam: A Reality or a Conspiracy Theory?', at the official website of Khamenei, the supreme leader of Iran, 15 July 2018 <https://english.khamenei.ir/news/5798/Cultural-invasion-on-Islam-a-reality-or-a-conspiracy-theory> [accessed 24 January 2023].

[9]   Khomeini wrote the following in his decree establishing the Cultural Revolution Headquarters on 12 June 1980: 'It is for some time the need for cultural revolution — that is an Islamic issue requested by the Muslim nation — has been highlighted but little has been done in this regard. The Muslim nation, especially the faithful and dedicated university students are concerned about this. They have also expressed concerns on sabotage of the conspirators, instances of which raises its head now and then. The Muslim nation are worried the chance might be missed without any positive work, so that the culture might remain the same as in the past corrupt regime. During the past regime, this fundamentally important center had been put at the disposal of the colonial powers by uncultured and uneducated employers. Sustainability of this

into a war in the cultural field with scholars as its generals. He stressed the need to return to the authentic roots of humanities and social sciences to avoid the influence of the West on Iranian students. Indeed, nativism in knowledge production is the official policy of higher education in Iran. The cultural invasion discourse, among others, renders a victim subject called Iran in that it focuses on global power relations at the expense of covering colonial relations between the national state and its 'margins' within the country.

Thinking about the politics of knowledge production means mapping our research onto the power structure dominating the very context of that production. Then, the geography or cognitive site we are referring to should be at the heart of our problematization, which is to say, in the case of Iran, it should be toward 'there' and not 'here'. By this, we primarily mean mapping out the power matrices that form the context of knowledge production 'there' and reflecting on the politics of scale in its historical problematization. For, if we start from 'here', a problematization about Iran remains captive to Northern perspectives, maybe even for the sake of addressing the expectations of Northern markets of knowledge production. In this context, one finds that the quest to discover anti-colonial figures and contributions has often ended with the same Islamist/nativist figures — the usual suspects. In the Global North, what is considered to be 'the authentic' Iran is often reduced to a 'cultural' narrative that, most of the time,

---

catastrophe that is the wish of some groups affiliated to foreign powers, will send a deadly shock throughout the Islamic Revolution and Islamic Republic of Iran. Any moderation in this vital issue is a grave treachery against Islam and against this Muslim country.' See the official website of the Supreme Council of the Cultural Revolution (SCCR) <https://sccr.ir/pages/10257/2> [accessed 24 January 2023].

is equivalent to the 'Islamic', too. In short, it should not be enough to go back to the same affiliated figures and rebrand them as decolonial contributors. Although such a gesture escapes the official colonial Islamist narrative of these figures/concepts, it does not allow for a deeper exploration of these figures promoted by the current regime in Iran and of other marginal figures overlooked by institutions in the Global North.[10]

IRANIAN STUDIES AND INSENSITIVITY TO THE PERIPHERY

Another example of the dominant paradigm of knowledge production on and through Iran concerns the importance and centrality of Iranian studies. We refer to Iranian studies as established area studies in North American and European academia to discuss how this institution has refashioned or even advanced, in some instances, the cognitive Southern-Northern division about the Iranian territory in Anglophone academia. Our focus, however, is on those works and scholars of Iranian studies who, working in the margins of the Global North, are critical of the orientalist gaze and adopt postcolonial and/or decolonial approaches in addressing their main subjects of study.

Before delving into that, let us briefly describe the demographic context of modern Iran. The current territory of Iran is home to diverse sociolinguistic and ethnic communities, which also include different religious groups. Farsi (Persian), the official language of Iran, which

---

10 For instance, Majid Rahnema, who criticizes the reproduction of co-
    lonial relations that takes place through the myth of development, is
    an example of those whose contributions have less often appeared in
    the quest to find anti-colonial figures in the so-called Global South. See
    Majid Rahnema and Victoria Bawartree, *The Post-development Reader*
    (London: Zed Books, 1997).

is politically and geographically associated with the central and eastern parts of the country, is the mother tongue of around sixty per cent of Iranian citizens. Farsi's history of domination as the national language of Iran coincides with the formation and centralization of Iran as a national state in the aftermath of the dissolution of the Persian empire, which took place along with the ethnicization and linguistic divisions that occurred under the watchful eyes of colonial powers and their administrators. The spatial implication of the centralization of the modern state was and still vividly is the constant accumulation of power, capital, science, and technology in the dominantly Farsi-speaking centre of Iran, particularly its capital Tehran. It also parallelly resulted in the marginalization and exclusion of the rest of the territory, i.e., the former frontier zones of the Persian empire, where the majority of non-Farsi speakers and many religiously non-Shia Muslims are located.

This has led us to ask: Who have been the subjects and objects of social research in so-called Iranian studies? Who has written the modern history of Iran? Who has imposed a certain order on its archive? Who has had the privilege to be represented as the Iranian people? The answer is: it has been predominantly the male Persian Shia figure. This is also the very same figure/subject that Iranian studies have mostly reproduced, even in their critical versions.[11]

---

11   For a few examples, please visit these prominent critical historical works that, despite addressing the others (e.g., ethnic, religious, and gendered others) of Iranian nationalism, have failed to integrate these others into their accounts of Iranian modernity: *Poetry and Revolution: The Poets and Poetry of the Constitutional Era of Iran*, ed. by Homa Katouzian and Alireza Korangi (London: Taylor & Francis, 2022); Homa Katouzian, *Iranian History and Politics: The Dialectic of State and Society* (London: Routledge, 2012); Abbas Amanat, *Iran: A Modern History* (New Haven, CT: Yale University Press, 2017); Mohammad Tavakoli-Targhi, *Refashioning Iran: Orientalism, Occidentalism and Historiography* (London: Palgrave, 2001).

While women's and gender studies in the past two decades, more or less, have been successful in releasing themselves from the gaze of heteronormative and male-dominated historical narratives, many of the works in Iranian studies and its broader institution, i.e., Middle Eastern studies, are still insensitive about the peripheries of Iran and the very processes of ethnic and religious marginalization. In other words, one can recognize systemic indifference and, in many instances, cognitive ignorance or suppression of non-male, non-Persian, non-Shia Iranians within the domain of Iranian studies. For instance, we reviewed most of the articles published in the past ten years in the journal of Iranian studies, which belongs to the Association for Iranian studies and is the most prestigious Anglophone journal in this area. Through our findings, we are surprised to realize that the peripheries and, more importantly, the 'peripheralization' of the national territory of Iran have barely appeared in analyses of Iranian modernity,[12] be it about subjects as diverse as development, nationalism, authoritarianism, or sexuality.

It should at least be noted that in the past decade, Iran has growingly witnessed political unrest and social protests in its peripheries, in the most marginalized neighbourhoods of both its cities and its provinces. Looking at, for instance, the geographical distribution and frequency of demonstrations in the current revolutionary movement and in the previous one in 2019 in Iran, one can see how their cartography is in line with the map of the most marginalized groups and peripheralized spaces of the country. The legacy of the political turmoil and revolutions in the

---

12   By 'peripheralization', we mean the mechanisms of constant centralization of knowledge and power in specific spaces and the parallel subjugation and suppression of other spaces and localities.

Middle East and the consequences of recent protests in Iran have inspired young scholars, mostly within Iran's isolated academic sphere or outside academia, to revise and reclaim the history of Iran and the Middle East differently by writing from and through the peripheries or, better to say, the Southern sites of the national state of Iran. However, we argue that these legacies have not yet been transferred or translated within the domain of English-speaking Iranian studies.

Instead, we recognize two important reactions in Iranian studies to the ongoing conflicts and struggles of peripheries against the core, as well as to the confrontation of the new political and discursive frame of the Middle East after the so-called Arab Spring:

1. The Persianate Studies Approach

This first approach has departed from Middle Eastern or Iranian studies in response to the critiques of the modernization theory in the Global North and is inspired by Shmuel Noah Eisenstadt's concept of 'multiple modernities'.[13] For its accounts of modernity, it focuses on civilizational analysis and the collective identities of the global periphery,[14] in this case, the Persianate region.[15] For

---

13   *Comparative Civilizations and Multiple Modernities*, ed. by Shmuel Noah Eisenstadt (Leiden: Brill, 2003); Shmuel Noah Eisenstadt, 'Multiple Modernities', *Daedalus*, 129.1 (2000), pp. 1–29.

14   Said Amir Arjomand, 'Multiple Modernities and the Promise of Comparative Sociology', in *Worlds of Difference*, ed. by Said Amir Arjomand and Elisa P. Reis (London: Sage, 2013), pp. 15–39.

15   These are examples of the first approach: *The Persianate World: Rethinking a Shared Sphere*, ed. by Abbas Amanat and Assef Ashraf (Leiden: Brill, 2018); Said Amir Arjomand, 'A Decade of Persianate Studies', *Journal of Persianate Studies*, 8.2 (2015), pp. 309–33; Said Amir Arjomand, 'From the Editor: Defining Persianate Studies', *Journal of Persianate Studies*, 1.1 (2008), pp. 1–4; Mohammad Tavakoli-Targhi,

Persianate scholars, this civilizational frame, provided by Persianate studies, is a convincing field of research against 'the divisive forces of modern nationalism, Islamic fundamentalism and imperialism'.[16] The initiators of Persianate studies justify the necessity of this field by stating that in contrast to Middle Eastern studies and Iranian studies, which are by-products of colonialism and nationalism, Persianate studies claim an objective and historically authentic and interdisciplinary field of knowledge production about a transnational entity, i.e., the Persianate world.[17] Thus, they claim that the ideal form of Persianate studies is free of methodological nationalism,[18] and that it provides 'the resources for decolonizing ourselves, for envisioning a future outside the heritage of European colonialism'.[19]

Despite its success in discussing similarities and 'longue durée commonalities' among South Asia, Central Asia, and Iran in a transnational framework,[20] Persianate studies, in some instances, reveal an imperial desire and tendency by some of its advocates to revive the glory of the pasts by assigning Persianate heritage in literature, culture, governance, and thoughts to certain people and places in nationalist discourses, notably in

---

'Early Persianate Modernity', in *Forms of Knowledge in Early Modern Asia: Explorations in the Intellectual History of India and Tibet, 1500–1800*, ed. by Sheldon Pollock (Durham, NC: Duke University Press, 2011), pp. 257–87; and Tavakoli-Targhi, *Refashioning Iran*.

16 Arjomand, 'Defining Persianate Studies', p. 4.

17 The Persianate world refers to a vast region that 'stretched from China to the Balkans, and from Siberia to southern India', where Persian was the main 'language of governance or learning'. See Nile Green, *The Persianate World: The Frontiers of a Eurasian Lingua Franca* (Berkeley: University of California Press, 2019), p.1.

18 Ibid., p.2.

19 Mana Kia, *Persianate Selves: Memories of Place and Origin before Nationalism* (Redwood City, CA: Stanford University Press, 2020), p. 4.

20 Assef Ashraf, 'Introduction: Pathways to the Persianate', in Amanat and Ashraf, *The Persianate World*, pp. 1–14 (p. 1).

Iran and India.[21] Furthermore, Persianate studies have
not offered a path towards making sense of the current
conjuncture, notably as far as mobility and mobilization
in and across different geopolitically important regions,
including the Middle East, are concerned. Indeed, as
Mana Kia rightfully puts it, 'reconceptualisation [and
denationalization/decolonization] requires self-reflexive
engagement with our own time and place.'[22] For instance,
Persianate scholars mainly depart from Iranian or
Middle Eastern studies by shifting their analytical focus
and interest towards a new cognitive site and broader
historical entity, the Persianate world. Yet, this does
not allow them to ignore the current political crisis and
core-periphery divisions in Iran and beyond. Nonetheless,
the dominant Persianate studies continue to undermine
the existence of both conflicts and commonalities in
the Middle Eastern context by attributing them to the
heritages of nationalism, colonialism/imperialism, and
political Islam. [23]

2. The Common Past(s) Approach

The second reaction to the intensification of the processes
of mobility and mobilization on the regional scale, in contrast, builds upon the idea of the common past(s) in the
Middle East and beyond, as well as on the possibility
of their restoration. This integrative approach emphasizes
what we know as 'cosmopolitan worldliness' as a strategy to

---

21   Kia, *Persianate Selves;* Green, *The Persianate World;* and Ashraf, 'Intro-
     duction: Pathways'.

22   Kia, *Persianate Selves*, p. 15.

23   In recent years, many have intuitively felt that those commonalities
     refer to a shared destiny more than to the sharing of a (imaginative)
     past.

understand social movements, regional conflicts, and civil war conditions,[24] and to criticize the processes of ethnicization and racialization as part of the colonial legacies in the Middle East and neighbouring regions. In his earlier book, *The Arab Spring: The End of Postcolonialism*, Hamid Dabashi argued for the emergence of a new world characterized by cosmopolitan worldliness in the aftermath of the early phases of the so-called Arab Spring and the overthrow of a few authoritarian regimes in the region.[25] For him, cosmopolitan worldliness 'has always been innate to these societies and is now being retrieved with a purposeful intent toward the future. This purposeful retrieval I call liberation geography'.[26]

In Dabashi's later book, *Iran Without Borders: Towards a Critique of the Postcolonial Nation*, this project of retrieving liberation geography emboldens the emancipatory potential beyond national borders and even criticizes methodological nationalism along with the marginalization of the former frontiers of empires. For Dabashi, the recent Middle Eastern revolutionary movements, including the Green movement of 2009 in Iran, transcend both colonial and postcolonial experiences by retrieving cosmopolitan worldliness. Indeed, these movements produce a new regime of knowledge that, according to him, 'decentre[s] the world and overcome[s] "the West" as a master trope of European modernity'.[27]

While the post-Arab Spring regime of knowledge production that is suggested by Dabashi acknowledges the

---

24   Hamid Dabashi, *Iran without Borders: Towards a Critique of the Postcolonial Nation* (London: Verso Books, 2016).

25   Hamid Dabashi, *The Arab Spring: The End of Postcolonialism* (London: Bloomsbury Publishing, 2012).

26   Ibid., p. 14.

27   Dabashi, *Iran without Borders*, p. 125.

Southern-Northern division within postcolonial states in the region and within Iranian borders, it shifts the temporality from the present to the past. For instance, the book implicitly claims that all of the different tensions and ongoing conflicts in the post-revolutionary moment of the region are historically 'imported conflicts' from the colonial powers or results of the malfunction of postcolonial states. Thus, cognitive preference is again given to utopian cosmopolitan pasts on a regional scale, as evident in Dabashi's insistence on the 'purposeful retrieval of [the] liberation geography' of the precolonial Middle East. However, this focus on the essentialized past overlooks the task of illuminating the ongoing processes of cognitive peripheralization and silencing imposed by post-Arab Spring national states in the region, which have led to further ethnicization or racialization on subnational and translocal scales.

To sum up, despite its progressive and decolonizing/denationalizing claims to promote liberation geography, the 'cosmopolitan worldliness' approach, as developed by Dabashi, cannot actualize the critical capacity of postcolonial critiques due to its focus on utopian past(s) and civilizational analysis, as similarly happens with Persianate studies.

CONCLUSION: OVERCOMING THE COGNITIVE
SOUTH-NORTH DIVISION

Returning to the problematic of this essay, one of the crucial demands of knowledge production in, from, and through the South(s) would be to shed light on the dual processes of centralization/marginalization or, in more political-economic sensitive terms, of peripheralization in line with the cognitive South-North division. However, at least in the context of Iranian studies, as discussed above, we are currently witnessing how localities and subnational peripheries, as Southern sites of knowledge production, are sacrificed and reduced to data-gathering zones in the name of resisting and undoing the very same mechanism of South-North or core-periphery divisions on a global scale. Therefore, we elaborate here on the importance of thinking about scale and the power asymmetries involved in knowledge production. At the same time, we aim to show how knowledge production can have different consequences and effects depending on scale.

What are the consequences of the kind of knowledge production on Iran that only stresses and takes into account transnational hierarchies and power structures, i.e., North-South divisions on a global scale? We suggest that it brings forward a relatively homogenizing account of Iran and, therefore, of a part of the Global South(s), which is, at best, methodologically nationalist and, at worst, politically nationalist and exclusionist. Thus, these accounts ignore the extreme hierarchies, cognitive injustices, and evidently harsh discriminations on other scales (regional, national, and subnational) that have day-by-day advanced ethnic conflicts, racism, sexism, and xenophobia within and beyond the national borders. In so doing, such accounts contribute to spreading these tensions across the region. Thus, focusing on a global scale of hierarchies, in this case, overlooks, if not obscures, power relations involved on a smaller scale.

Let us conclude our contribution with some suggestions as to how to address some of the main questions put forth by this volume:

First, since part of the problem we have raised here has been inherited from the legacy of area studies, we propose to address this institutional structure directly. Area studies in general are deeply entangled with colonial histories and continue to serve the extractivist approach to knowledge production. As we have argued, they suit the interests of both national states and regional powers. While being aware that area studies and the discursive prisons they produce cannot be dissolved overnight, what we can do is to critically reflect on their claims and functions. We need to understand them as a site of intervention for decolonizing the above-described power asymmetries involved in hegemonic modes of knowledge production. Within this frame, we should take both the critiques of methodological nationalism and the politics of scale seriously. By the latter, we mean how the dominant scales of problematization are constructed and reproduced, as well as the power struggles that form the context in which it takes place. In this sense, far from being merely a methodological choice in a voluntarist sense, scale is a historical construct with a specific power matrix as its context.

Our bringing forth the politics of scale as a contested site of intervention aims at resisting the logic of othering underlying the South-North division. This binary thinking not only overlooks South-South efforts and affinities but also fosters the further peripheralization of marginalized sites and subjects even within those contexts. For example, Baluch Sunni females are as crucial as other figures in conceiving Iranian modern history. The processes of marginalization and exclusion of such subjects must be revisited if the histories of the national states in the Middle East are to be written differently. This sensitivity to power structures might even contribute to transforming the research agenda of area studies. As already mentioned, problematization must come from 'there' as the site where knowledge is produced, not from 'here' as the institutions where the Global South(s) is consumed and conceptualized.

Our second concern goes beyond the specific field of area studies. It is broadly an epistemological concern and aims to overcome insensitivity to the peripheries in our effort to theorize through and from the Global South(s). We, therefore, adopt Edward Said's conceptualization of anti-orientalism as 'a decentered consciousness'.[28] We can and should nurture a decentred consciousness to confront potential cognitive division and peripheralization in the process of knowledge production in and through the Global South(s). In this regard, feminist contributions to the relationality of what we define as the South or, better to say, the South(s), are very crucial. As Amy Piedalue and Susmita Rishi have noted, we need to view the 'south as a flexible and mobile marker that draws our gaze to the operation of Imperial power, manifest in complex inequalities articulated at local and global scales'.[29] In this sense, they argue that 'theorising from the South' requires 'a kind of counter-mapping that centralizes the insights and theories that emerge from positions of struggle and marginality'.[30]

This brings us to our last point: ethical/political concerns. Regardless of their scale and space, social struggles and emancipatory politics must guide us to evaluate how we decentre our consciousness to problematize and theorize in, through, and from the South(s). That said, perhaps we need native problematization and universal inspiration in order to develop the fresh perspectives that Asef Bayat suggests and to change two interconnected things

---

28   Edward W. Said, 'Orientalism Reconsidered', *Cultural Critique*, 1 (1985), pp. 89–107.

29   Amy Piedalue and Susmita Rishi, 'Unsettling the South through Postcolonial Feminist Theory', *Feminist Studies*, 43.3 (2017), pp. 548–70 (p. 555).

30   Ibid., p. 569.

simultaneously:[31] first, our understanding of the Global South(s), and second, the relations between the Global South(s) and the Global North(s).

---

31   Asef Bayat, *Life as Politics: How Ordinary People Change the Middle East* (Redwood City, CA: Stanford University Press, 2013), p. 5.

Invitation, To Exi(s)t

IRACEMA DULLEY AND JULIANA M. STREVA

Iracema: This joint piece aspires to be a dialogue. In a dialogue, people speak and, most importantly, listen, from their respective positions. It can take the form of questions and answers, of a jointly developed train of thought, of respect in disagreement, of fragmentation. Openness is a fundamental key: to discovery, to difference, to the other's desire. Dialogues do not always happen. But we strive.

Juliana: Indeed, a fragmented and yet persistent dialogue. In response to what you just said, Iracema, we could perhaps speculate on the very notion of dialogue. We are not at a bar now, but we could still imagine a Brazilian *boteco*, the kind of sidewalk bar where we have the most unexpected kinds of conversation, right?

Iracema: Agreed. And since this is the work of imagination, it should be sunny.

Juliana: A sunny afternoon it is. And we are sitting on red plastic chairs while sharing some fried manioc. With this scenario in mind, I can follow up on my initial divagation on the concept of dialogue. The fact that a dialogue involves both the act of speaking and the act of listening is a relevant point of departure that should not be taken for granted. It reminds me of a performative exercise proposed by Grada Kilomba in which she invites the audience to speak at the same time that she does, and asks: 'Would I still have the authority as the speaker?'. Afterwards, she concludes that '[l]istening is, in a sense, like an act of authorization towards the speaker. One can only speak when one's voice is listened to'.[1]

Moreover, speaking is not merely the sonic vibration of one's voice. The notion of voice encompasses not only the oral sound, but also the voice in the form of written expression and the corporeal performative gestures conceptualized by Leda Maria Martins as *oralitura*.[2] Instead of reinforcing the colonial binary hierarchization of the written over the oral form, I follow Martins in addressing them in relation: the speaker and the writer, the act of listening, and the act of reading. Therefore, speaking-writing refers to a relational movement that is possible only when listening-reading is its counterpart.

---

1   In her piece 'Decolonising Knowledge', Grada Kilomba described her interaction with the audience as very shy. I imagine that the audience might not have spoken loudly enough to create a proper cacophony that would have prevented Kilomba's voice from being heard through a microphone. Nevertheless, it still worked as an exercise. Cf. Grada Kilomba, 'Decolonising Knowledge', in *The Struggle Is Not Over Yet: An Archive in Relation*, ed. by Nuno Faria, Filipa César, and Tobias Hering (Berlin: Archive Books, 2015), pp. 191–208 (p. 194).

2   By displacing the European rhetoric that privileges written archives over oral sources, Leda Maria Martins recalls how in one of the Bantu languages of the Congo, the verbs 'to write' and 'to dance' derive from the same root, *ntanga*. According to Martins, this makes reference to other possible sources of inscription, preservation, transmission, and transcription of knowledge, practices, and procedures anchored in and by the body in performance. Cf. Leda Maria Martins, *Afrografias da Memória* (São Paulo, Belo Horizonte: Perspectiva, Mazza Edições, 1997).

Three words have been appearing and reappearing in my thoughts, and even in my dreams: author, authority, and authoritarian. I became intrigued by the repetition of 'author' and decided to check the semantic roots of these words. The term 'author' comes from the Latin *auctor*, which refers to the promoter, producer, or founder, literally, the one who causes something to grow — *auctus* is the past participle of *augere* (to increase).

In my everyday interactions, the figure of the author is commonly understood as a way of naming the person who writes (*she is a writer, she is an author*). In the academic sphere, for instance, the acts of reading and writing have been granting authority to the figure of the author as the knowledge producer *par excellence*, who Trinh T. Minh-ha named the 'voice of knowledge'.[3] As I attempt to reassemble my train of thought in the form of speculative questions, the voice and the writer return in a spiral here. Since the birth of modern colonization until today, has the imbrication between author and authority been merely reduced to etymology? Or has it rather manifested itself in the form of material and historical entanglements that continually legitimize academic research in order to speak *about* or even *for* others (researched subjects, who have been violently framed as objects)? How can one liberate the act of speaking-writing from the colonial structures of othering and ownership that are continually reinscribed by the disciplinary system of knowledge? Far from aspiring to elict a how-to recipe in response, these questions are an invitation to interrogate (and unlearn) what we today know as theoretical knowledge, detached from the empirical and from experience, as well as to learn from and with

---

3   Trinh T. Minh-ha, *Woman, Native, Other: Writing Postcoloniality and Feminism* (Bloomington: Indiana University Press, 1989), p. 63.

the continual insurgent attempts at thinking, moving, listening, and speaking *nearby*.[4]

Iracema: I was drawn to both anthropology and psychoanalysis because I wanted to answer an impossible question: What do others think? Anthropology and psychoanalysis have historically provided an explanation for otherness: in terms of sociocultural and psychic difference, historical development, or positionality within a structure. Through categories such as culture, structure, society, subject, or symptom, they attempt to circumscribe difference. Such differences are, as I have argued elsewhere, constituted in the very act of their naming. For, as Jacques Derrida reminds us, names precede and exceed what they name.[5] In anthropology, units of analysis have been traditionally constituted through the emic gesture, which consists of the act of naming the difference to be described.[6] In (Lacanian) psychoanalysis, the unit of analysis is the subject that emerges in relation to a chain of signifiers.[7] Units of analysis are fictive, for the borders that constitute them are the product of implicit theory, that is, of disciplinary common sense. This is not to say that differences do not exist. They do. But their existence is inseparable from the

---

4   Trinh T. Minh-ha, '"Speaking Nearby": A Conversation with Trinh T. Minh-ha', *Visual Anthropology Review*, 8.1 (1992), pp. 82–91. These gestures attempt to not be equated with what Jota Mombaça describes as the benevolent narratives of the white alliance, perpetuated within the formulas of 'giving space', 'giving visibility', and 'giving voice'. Cf. Mombaça, *Não Vão Nos Matar Agora* (Rio de Janeiro: Cobogó, 2021), pp. 38–40.

5   Jacques Derrida, 'Plato's Pharmacy', in *Dissemination*, trans. by Barbara Johnson (Chicago: University of Chicago Press, 1981), pp. 61–171.

6   See Iracema Dulley, *On the Emic Gesture: Difference and Ethnography in Roy Wagner* (London: Routledge, 2019).

7   Iracema Dulley develops this further in 'The Case and the Signifier: Generalization in Freud's Rat Man', in *The Case for Reduction*, ed. by Christoph F. E. Holzhey and Jakob Schillinger (Berlin: ICI Berlin Press, 2022), pp. 13–37.

processes through which they are named — processes in which authorship and authority become imbricated. Differences in the world are inseparable from differences in language. And yet, the relationship between language and the world is one of displacement.

One can only have access to the thoughts of others through what they say. The invitation to speak, think, and listen *nearby*, proposed by Trinh T. Minh-ha, has to do with the recognition that the language of others, in whatever form, will remain opaque to us.[8] There is no possible method through which one could claim to know what others actually think. And yet, one can listen to them, talk to them, and think about what one has heard from them. In short, one can listen to what others say without claiming to understand and represent them, which would be tantamount to speaking *for* them, the ultimate colonial gesture. Rather, when one speaks *nearby*, one can speak and be heard from a position that does not aspire to authority. The opacity of others can be uncanny because it reminds us of a more elementary opacity: that of the language in and through which subjects are constituted. For one knows very well that there is always a gap between what one does say and what one wishes one could formulate. If one cannot be equal to oneself as one speaks, how could one expect to speak for and about others?

Colonial discourse reiteratively misrecognizes its own epistemic (in)capacities whenever it claims to speak for others. Whenever academic discourse does the same, it reinstates a colonial gesture. The reason why such a claim is not understood to be delusional is that it is uttered from a position of authority. This is especially relevant when one thinks of the relationship between theorization and the places that are now fashionably said to pertain to the Global South (be-

---

8   Trinh, 'Speaking Nearby'.

fore they were given other names: periphery, third world, the margins). Theory aims at generalization, which is a significant process if one wants to make abstract claims — a process that is necessary for politics, ethics, and science. Yet, theory frequently dismisses its vernacular expressions either as minor instantiations of its greater potential for abstraction or as mere examples for its proof or disproof. In view of this, we invite our readers to unsettle the distinction between theory (what has historically been understood to be produced in the Global North) and the empirical, the 'stuff' or 'matter' to which it is related (what has historically taken place just anywhere, that is, both in the Global North and in the Global South). From this perspective, ethnography is understood to provide the empirical matter of anthropology, whereas the clinic does the same for psychoanalysis; the contents thus produced are expected to be analysed from the perspective of theories that have the North as their centre and reduce the South to the role of content provider. Thus, undoing the distinction between the theoretical and the empirical poses the possibility of knowledge produced in the Global South not only unsettling commonsensical assumptions held in the Global North, but also blurring the very divide between North and South, the general and the particular. If one undoes the hierarchy between the theoretical and the empirical, a space might emerge in which the very language of abstraction materializes in its opacity. In this sense, opacity is to be understood both in relation to the materiality of signifiers — whose coupling with signifieds remains unstable (an understanding of language shared by both Derrida and Lacan) — and as unquantifiable alterity, as proposed by Édouard Glissant. (As I understand it, this kind of alterity cannot be exoticized by acts of naming.)[9]

---

9   Édouard Glissant, *Poetics of Relation*, trans. by Betsy Wing (Ann Arbor: University of Michigan Press, 1990).

Juliana: Theory is indeed not essentially authoritarian, but *can* be performed in an oppressive manner. This happens when it is designed to maintain the existing power relations, or used to exert authority, as in the obvious cases of social Darwinism and supposedly scientific racist theories. But not only in these cases. The traditional, 'objective', and Eurocentric definitions of knowledge and scientific methods have persistently employed theory in order to legitimize extractivist regimes and structural privileges. As Denise Ferreira da Silva highlights, this is because the 'arsenal designed to determine and to ascertain the truth of human difference already assumed Europeanness/whiteness as the universal measure'.[10] By naming the author as the expert, the Western system of knowledge consolidated the figure of the author as authority, as if writing were not necessarily a relational exercise of tacit or explicit dialogue. Who has historically embodied this author/ity position?

Instead of opening and broadening the conversation, as suggested by the semantics of *auctus*, academia, in its colonial genealogy of existence, has historically perpetuated the monopolization and homogenization of the conditions of enunciation. Such a political economy of knowledge has produced a monologue, what Trinh designated 'scientific gossip',[11] in which one speaks about or for others, instead of speaking with them, as would be desired in a dialogue.[12]

---

10   Denise Ferreira da Silva , '1 (Life) ÷ 0 (Blackness) = $\infty - \infty$ or ∞ / ∞: On Matter Beyond the Equation of Value', *E-Flux Journal*, 79 (2017), p. 8 <http://worker01.e-flux.com/pdf/article_94686.pdf> [accessed 13 August 2023].

11   Trinh, *Woman, Native, Other*, p. 68.

12   On the concept of a 'political economy of knowledge', see Silvia Rivera Cusicanqui, 'Ch'ixinakax Utxiwa: A Reflection on the Practices and Discourses of Decolonization', in *Ch'ixinakax utxiwa: On Practices and*

Iracema: Embracing opacity is a possible strategy to challenge authority as the place from which one is certain about the knowledge that one supposedly possesses. In Lacanian terms, one speaks about the supposed subject of knowledge in relation to transference, that is, the analysand's belief that the analyst possesses a kind of knowledge about her that she herself does not.[13] Transference, which is fundamental for analysis to occur, rests on this supposition. Yet, whenever the analyst actually believes that she occupies this position of knowledge, hers becomes a position of narcissistic deafness, from which imaginary projections silence the opaque alterity that resides in the other's discourse. From the perspective from which one speaks, listens, and thinks nearby, however, the narcissistic 'I' is erased by the kind of invention that results from non-ego-based engagement with the imaginary, such as happens in dialogues or dreams. In this respect, it would be interesting to extend the notion of a supposed subject of knowledge to academic discourse. As one relinquishes the drive to possess knowledge, 'I' becomes the provisional, fictive, aspiring position from which desire can be ethically enunciated. For one desires the other's desire, which is unknown to oneself and does not conform to the projections of the imagined, narcissistic 'I'. From such a position, opacity sends us back to that which is material in language, in other words, that which resides beyond meaning and yet resonates and displaces it.[14]

Discourses of Decolonization, trans. Molly Geidel (Cambridge: Polity Press, 2010), p. 102.

13   Jacques Lacan, *The Four Fundamental Concepts of Psychoanalysis*, ed. by Jacques-Alain Miller, trans. by Alan Sheridan (London: Hogarth Press, 1971).

14   Iracema Dulley engages with these questions in more detail in 'The Voice in Rape', *European Journal of Psychoanalysis*, 9.2 (2022) <https://www.journal-psychoanalysis.eu/articles/the-voice-in-rape/>.

Juliana: *Isso!* The psychoanalytical figure of the sup-posed subject of knowledge has also been elaborated by Lélia Gonzalez, who worked on and displaced this Lacan-ian concept. In view of whiteness as a structure of power, Gonzalez proposes a racialized reading of the figure of the supposed subject of knowledge as a means of unsettling the fabrication of what she calls 'internal colonialism'.[15] A few weeks ago, I was writing precisely on Gonzalez's extension of the notion of a supposed subject of knowledge to aca-demic discourse.[16]

Iracema: I was thinking of how the supposed sub-ject of knowledge, whose position can be imaginarily con-ceived as that of the old, white, male academic who holds a professorship, can be undone by embracing the void. Maybe one can think of the void as one of the possible instantiations of opacity. In 'The Plural Void: Barthes and Asia', Trinh T. Minh-ha and Stanley Gray seek inspiration in Barthes's understanding of writing as a kind of *satori* to dwell on the loss of meaning that is necessary for writing as that which is based on a 'speech-void'.[17] The void can receive names and yet remain devoid of meaning, for it is matte, opaque. The relationship between language and the world or its experience is mediated, which is to say

---

15   Lélia Gonzalez, 'Por Um Feminismo Afro-Latino-Americano', in *Por Um Feminismo Afro-Latino-Americano*, ed. by Flavia Rios and Márcia Lima (Rio de Janeiro: Zahar, 1988), pp. 139–50 (p. 142).

16   Reverberating Frantz Fanon's notion of sociogeny, I engage in the men-tioned paper with Lélia Gonzalez's (re)conceptions of the Lacanian terms of the *infans* and the supposed subject of knowledge as a gesture that both renders suspicious the a priori defined social roles of subjects of knowledge and disputes what has been defined as valid, legitim-ate, and 'scientific' knowledge. Juliana M. Streva, 'Fugitive Dialogues: Speaking Nearby Lélia Gonzalez and Frantz Fanon', *Philosophy and Global Affairs Journal* (forthcoming, 2024).

17   Trinh T. Minh-ha and Stanley Gray, 'The Plural Void: Barthes and Asia', *SubStance*, 11.3 (1982), pp. 41–50 <https://doi.org/10.2307/3684313>.

that it is indirect. Trinh and Gray remind us of Barthes's admonition against treating directly a structure that functions through indirection. In so doing, it either 'escapes, it empties out, or on the contrary, it freezes, essentializes'.[18] When talking about this structure that basically demands to be engaged with through indirection, Barthes gives a name to what he phrases as the reservoir of empty signs that allows for indirection: Japan. His reflection on the undecidable nature of the relationship between the signifier and the signified, form and content, is shaped by this name. It is as if Japan could provisionally stand for indirection and undecidability. In this reductive move, Japan stands simultaneously for a structure to be opposed to the structure in which the (Western) author originally operates and for the kind of structure towards which one should strive. This proposition is not devoid of totalizing exoticization. And yet, Barthes also claims that writing 'undoes nomination',[19] the logical consequence of this affirmation being the undoing of the juxtaposition between the name Japan and the structure of indirection with which it is juxtaposed.

If in writing one embraces the void of language, one also undoes the authority, authorship, and authoritarianism that are associated with the position of the 'I' as that of the supposed subject of knowledge, understood as the sovereign originator of discourse. From the perspective of colonial anthropology, the position of authority is one from which the author claims to state what is and what is not Japan. Yet, in writing, one allows oneself to be estranged in and through language. As Trinh and Gray put it, 'the ego-mirror is the equivalent of a polite host who allows "thousands of subjects" to make themselves at home

---

18   Quoted in ibid., p. 41.
19   Ibid., p. 43.

in his dwelling and to speak through him. His/her portrait, structural and non-psychological, dramatizes an *utterance* (*énonciation*).'[20] Maybe this is, as such, the condition of possibility for dialogue to happen.

With this invitation, we strive for the kind of dialogue that happens between structurally positioned writing subjects who, while acknowledging their place in a given structure, do not fiercely identify themselves with a privileged position and allow for the language of the other to displace them. Of course, words alone will not do the work of transformation that is needed to surpass structural inequalities, authoritarianism, and the supposition of knowledge. This kind of transformation often involves and even requires confrontational gestures, since the holders of privilege do not usually relinquish and share them willingly. But since we are giving free rein to our imagination, let us embrace utopia for a change. In the kind of dialogue we aspire to, writers 'for[m] and [are] formed by a layering and separation of the 'I' [...] a plurality of subjects of speaking and of speech, and of the denunciation of these'.[21] As such, invaded by language and the possibilities it entails and forecloses, the writer is and is not the void. The writer aspires to go beyond the name that grants authority as she merges with language.

Juliana: She merges with language... Resonating with what you just said on the subject of the writer, I find it both poetic and political how Trinh reads the act of writing as a process of becoming. Diverging from the idea of becoming a writer or a poet, she conceives of becoming as an intransitive verb: to become. The process of becoming is said to take place only when the writer 'traces for itself

---

20   Ibid., p. 48.
21   Ibid.

lines of evasion.'[22] In her work, these lines are presented as an excursion, the act of walking that could take one where one is not expected to be, a speculative movement with no fixed trajectory, formula, or prescriptive procedure to be mechanically applied.

Perhaps these lines of evasion have the potentiality to reverberate an even more radical gesture than that of a mere excursion. Here, I hear the echo of Frantz Fanon's words: 'I leave methods to the botanists and the mathematicians. There is a point at which methods devour themselves. I should like to start from there.'[23] In my view, these lines should not be disconnected from the anticolonial tactics of fugitivity, of escaping, and of refusing the ontological and epistemic pact imposed by colonialism.[24] Differently from a metaphor or a utopia, it designates a historical praxis that is a continuum. As we learn from Beatriz Nascimento, *quilombo* fugitivity in the context of slavery and its aftermath should not be understood as the incapacity to fight or as an event constrained by the past.[25] *Quilombo* fugitivity refers

---

22   Trinh, *Woman, Native, Other*, p. 31.

23   Frantz Fanon, *Black Skin, White Masks* [1952], trans. by Charles Lam Markmann (New York: Pluto Press, 1986), p. 14.

24   Streva engages with the notion of the pact in more detail in Juliana M. Streva, Ana Luiza Braga, and Lior Zalis, 'Speculating Pacts on the Common', *La Escuela* (2022) <https://laescuela.art/en/campus/library/mappings/speculating-pacts-on-the-common-ana-luiza-braga-juliana-streva-and-lior-zisman-zalis>.

25   Beatriz Nascimento, 'Transcrição do Documentário Orí [1989]', in *Beatriz Nascimento. Quilombola e Intelectual. Possibilidade nos Dias da Destruição*, ed. by União dos Coletivos Pan-Africanistas (Diáspora Africana: Editora Filhos da África, 1989), pp. 326–40 (p. 329). Historically, these ancestral strategies have been protagonized by Afro-diasporic persons who created *quilombos*, involving also Amerindian peoples and a few poor white persons, in order to live otherwise in the plantation system. Spread throughout the territory today known as Brazil, *quilombo* refers to Afro-diasporic communities confronting and resisting colonial-slavery regimes. Across the Americas, they are also known as *cumbes, palenques, mambises, ladeiras, bush negroes, cimarrones, cima-*

to an ancestral and ongoing practice of radical contestation of the colonial order and to the organization of other ways of living together. In a system in which there is no way out, fugitive gestures take place from the inside.

Glissant remarks that 'the writer, entering the dense mass of his writings, renounces an absolute, his poetic intention, full of self-evidence and sublimity', and that '[t]he text passes from a dreamed of transparency to the opacity produced in words.'[26] Author, authority, authoritarian. The attempt to speak and listen nearby is not equivalent with losing one's voice or remaining in silence. For the act of listening, silence is crucial. But absolute silence can also entail the absence of dialogue, engagement, and response. It might even express the convenience of retaining privilege or imposing authority. In striving for dialogue, there is the possibility of displacing theory and unsettling colonial legacies. In short, of exi(s)ting together.

Iracema: Yes, this is how we started this conversation: an invitation to exit is sometimes an invitation to exist.

~

This is a fragment of an ongoing dialogue. So let its closure be an opening to what is to come.

Our epigraph comes at the end:

'The closure here, however, is a way of letting the work go rather than of sealing it off.'[27]

---

ronaje, marronages, and maroons. Cf. Gonzalez, 'Por Um Feminismo Afro-Latino-Americano', pp. 76–79.

26   Glissant, *Poetics of Relation*, p. 115.

27   Trinh T. Minh-ha, *When the Moon Waxes Red: Representation, Gender and Cultural Politics* (New York: Routledge, 1991).

To Be Given Names
Displaced Social Positionalities in Senegal and Angola

IRACEMA DULLEY AND FREDERICO SANTOS DOS SANTOS

INTERSECTIONALITY AND VERNACULAR FORMS OF INTERPELLATION

It is by now widely accepted in the social sciences and beyond that the positionality of subjects in the world is overdetermined by their social placement through markers such as race, class, and gender. Within this picture, intersectionality studies make visible that intersectional crossings between these categorizations further overdetermine the possibilities of action and experience of social subjects.[1]

---

1   The term intersectionality was coined by Kimberle Crenshaw in 'Mapping the Margins: Intersectionality, Identity Politics, and Violence Against Women of Color', *Stanford Law Review*, 43.6 (1991), pp. 1241–99. A non-exhaustive list of works inspiring our engagement with this subject includes Angela Davis, *Women, Race and Class* (New York: Random House, 1981); bell hooks, *Ain't I a Woman: Black Women and Feminism* (Boston: South End Press, 1981); Patricia Hill Collins, *Black Feminist Thought: Knowledge, Consciousness, and the Politics of Empowerment* (Boston: Hyman, 1990); and Audre Lorde, *The Black Unicorn* (New York: Norton and Company, 1995).

For instance, if subjects are by default assigned a hierarch-
ically inferior position in the world by the fact that they
were born a woman, further inequalities can result from
the addition of other social markers to this condition: If
one is not only a woman but also black and queer, one's
unequal placement is even greater. Intersectionality was
proposed by black feminist scholars whose positionality in
the world allowed them to formulate a critique not only of
racism but also of (white) feminism. Their critique of the
knowledge produced in ignorance of such overdetermin-
ations informs our thinking as we propose to complexify
the general categories employed in intersectionality studies through a consideration of local, vernacular forms of
interpellation.

On the one hand, we acknowledge the political and
epistemic value of the reduction performed by categorizations such as race, class, and gender due to their revelation
of the historical situatedness of the asymmetries that are inherent to power relations. On the other hand, we are faced
with the fact that we rarely find straightforward equivalents for such categories as we attempt to translate them
into non-academic, non-Anglophone contexts in the so-
called Global South where we develop our research as
anthropologists. Thus, we explore here the complicated
relationship between emplacement and translation as we
compare the names given to Iracema Dulley in Angola and
to Frederico Santos in Senegal. Whereas Iracema had her
personal name changed and was designated in Portuguese
as *branca* (white), *doutora* (doctor), and *irmã* (sister) and
in Umbundu as *ocindele*, Frederico was renamed Bamba
Fall by one of the families who hosted him and called a
toubab. What the terms *ocindele* and *toubab* have in common is that they are vernacular terms that simultaneously

hint at the positionality of the 'white' and the 'foreigner' but do not fully correspond to it.

Investigating the effects of such names and how they emplaced us during our fieldwork, we contend that understanding positionality also involves paying attention to how general categories are displaced in the process of their translation into local designators — in the cases addressed here, into Portuguese, Umbundu, and Wolof. It is certainly true that names such as *branca*, *ocindele*, and *toubab* point to intersectional positionality related to race, class, gender, and place of origin. Yet, reducing the names that one is given by others to such generalizing categories poses the risk of flattening out our understanding of the relationship between the gaze of others, the names they give us, and where this places us in relation to them. It is with this in mind that we propose to reflect on the implications of such acts of naming in the context of our fieldworks in Angola and Senegal. What follows engages with these questions: Towards what local social positions do the designations we were given gesture? What historicity is contained in the iterations of these names? What do they say about one's behaviour and about what is expected of one in a given situation? What contextual possibilities of action and experience do they allow for or foreclose? To what extent can one accept or reject them? What would be the consequences of doing so?

FIELDWORK: NAMING DISPLACEMENT

During fieldwork in Angola, Iracema was given many names. Her first name, Iracema, was often transformed into a local variant that she had never heard before: Iracelma. After repeating the correct pronunciation of her name a couple of times on different occasions to different people to no effect, she gave up and accepted the new name. Thus, whenever she heard that name, she knew it referred to her and responded to it. Despite the fact that she did not feel any connection to this new name and did not even like it, she understood that her actual name was unknown to her interlocutors and easily replaceable by a local name everyone seemed to recognize. Thus, in the process of being made more familiar to her interlocutors, she accepted to be further estranged from herself in language as she took on a name that sounded too similar to be someone else's and too strange to be her own.

Indeed, this might be a significant part of what field-work is about: engaging with one's perception of oneself (which includes one's self-image, one's supposed abilities, and the sound of one's name) through the gaze and speech of others as one realizes that one's self-perception is not confirmed by those one encounters. This is made visible in the process of transliteration of one's name, which some-times cannot be reproduced in a different phonetic sys-tem and symbolic environment. It is relevant to note that the transliteration of the name Iracema has happened not only in Angola, but also in different English-, French-, and German-speaking contexts. Transliteration is one way in which one's externality vis-à-vis a context that is different from the one in which one was originally named is marked at the moment of interpellation: Every time one is thus called, one is reminded of the fact that one's placement in a new context is always a kind of displacement. Transliter-ation indexes foreignness, otherness, and non-belonging.

Iracema was also assigned two status names during fieldwork: *doutora* and *irmã*. *Doutora* (a female doctor, in Portuguese) is the epithet by which she was frequently ad-dressed by those interlocutors who had first met her as a researcher. In Angola, it is not uncommon for those who

have completed a university degree to be called doctors
as a mark of distinction, even if they do not hold a PhD.
Therefore, the fact that she came from Brazil with a university degree to do research automatically placed her in this
position. This hierarchical, respectful form of address made
her uncomfortable, for she was used to being called by her
first name in both daily and academic situations elsewhere.
However, she accepted it as an accurate description of her
social position and responded to it. This was not devoid of
irony, for she was not always in the position of the expert
during her fieldwork. On many occasions, she was told to
consult elderly male authority figures who were considered
specialists in whatever was related to Umbundu expression.
They called her *doutora*, but she was the one learning from
them even though many of them did not hold an academic
degree.

On her first field trip to Huambo, Central Angola,
the nuns who hosted her also called her *irmã* (sister, in
Portuguese), a form of address that she inadvertently re-
ciprocated. The person who had found her a place to stay
and put her in touch with her hosts was a nun she had
met in Luanda. Given the fact that she had travelled alone
by bus from Luanda to Huambo and used to walk everywhere — something white foreigners rarely do in Angola
— she was mistaken for a nun on many occasions. It took
her some time to realize the misunderstanding. She finally
did so when asked questions about her congregation of
origin. Surprised, she explained to the nuns hosting her
that she was not one and pointed to the fact that she did not
wear religious clothing, to which her hosts replied that Brazilian nuns sometimes do not. Had she been a practicing
Catholic, she would have immediately understood that the
meaning of 'sister', in this context, had to do with belonging

to a religious community and not with a general feeling of openness and sorority.

Her positionality during fieldwork was marked by these two forms of address. In the first case, the status name she was given both distanced her from her interlocutors and assigned her the place from which her research became possible: the respected but distant position of the white intellectual who is supposed to be talking not to everyone but to the (elderly, male) authorities on the subject being investigated by her/him/them — a position that was not only ironic, but also restrictive of her interests, curiosity, and longing for horizontality. In suggesting who she was to talk to, her interlocutors influenced the kind of discourse she would be able to produce and reproduce. On one occasion, after an interview with an elder affiliated with the UNITA party,[2] his wife explicitly told her, 'Work for us, *doutora*!', despite Angolan politics not having been mentioned as a topic in their conversation. In the second case, the misunderstanding assigned her a comfortable place in the religious community at first, but then created an uncomfortable situation that finally became a joke.

---

2   Angola became independent from Portugal in 1975. In the wake of independence, the diplomatic attempt to divide the power of the state between the main anticolonial movements that had fought against colonialism failed. The MPLA (People's Movement for the Liberation of Angola) inherited the state from Portugal and started to rule the country from Luanda. This was almost immediately opposed by UNITA (National Movement for the Total Independence of Angola) and FNLA (National Liberation Front of Angola), giving rise to a civil war that lasted until 2002. During this period, UNITA, backed by the US and apartheid South Africa in the context of the Cold War, challenged the MPLA's claim to the state with the support of Cuba and the Soviet Union. Central Angola, where Umbundu is spoken and Iracema did her fieldwork, is the place of origin of Savimbi, UNITA's mythical leader, as well as of many of its officials. After the war ended, UNITA became a political party and remains a relevant force of opposition against MPLA rule until now.

The first name she was given depended on the adaptation of her first name to the pool of names commonly employed by her interlocutors, whereas the status names she received in Portuguese referred to something people either knew or assumed to know about her. The latter were given to her with respect and consideration. Yet, among the names one is called during fieldwork are not only direct forms of address; one might also overhear others speaking about oneself to other people, such as was the case with *ocindele*. On the one hand, the fact that she was white, or Brazilian, was directly mentioned as an explanation for her assumed lack of knowledge about certain local specificities (local diseases, culinary singularities, specific rituals, and practices related to witchcraft). On the other hand, given the fact that most white people cannot speak Umbundu, people usually felt at ease to talk about her as *ocindele* whenever they spoke Umbundu among themselves, for they assumed that she would not understand that they were referring to her.

Ocindele, a term that was translated as 'white' in the context of colonialism and the related process of racialization, points not only to one's skin colour, but also to one's wealth, position of privilege, and/or foreign status.[3] At the time when this translation was coined, Umbundu speakers employed *ocindele* both to designate the white merchants with whom they used to trade and to describe someone who was black but wealthy and behaved in a way considered foreign. Thus, in colonial sources, one finds black people who are said to be *ocindele* — due to their wealth, proximity to the colonizer, or estrangement from

---

3   On the translation of *ocindele* as 'white', see Iracema Dulley, 'Naming Others: Translation and Subject Constitution in the Central Highlands of Angola (1926–1961)', *Comparative Studies in Society and History*, 64.2 (2022), pp. 363–93.

local social ties. The juxtaposition of white merchants and local wealthy traders through this name points to the perception that they occupied a similar position in Central Angola before the establishment of colonial rule.[4] Iracema was called *ocindele* at first glance, based on her appearance. As a white woman, it would have been unlikely not to be called that. The fact that she was positioned as a white female researcher in the field overdetermined her possibilities of access and experience. Yet, this name cannot be equated with race alone, for it is as much about social status or class as it is about race. For instance, being white automatically creates the expectation that one should have the means and willingness to pay for transportation. This is what she learned as she listed to her Umbundu-speaking interlocutors. On one occasion, as she preferred walking home to taking a moto taxi, the driver deridingly told his colleague that 'the *ocindele* has no money'.

In Iracema's case, people talked about her behind her back because they imagined that an *ocindele* would not understand Umbundu. Supposing her deafness to their language, they marked her foreignness, her racial positionality, and her assumed social class without taking her presence into consideration. She could understand that she was being talked about only because she could understand their language. Yet, although *ocindele* and *toubab* point to a similar position and disposition related to whiteness and foreign status, in the case of Frederico it would not have been necessary for him to understand Wolof to notice that people were talking about him.

---

4   For an Umbundu account of the period that precedes and follows the establishment of colonial rule in Central Angola in the aftermath of the Bailundo War (1902–03), see Iracema Dulley, 'Chronicles of Bailundo: A Fragmentary Account in Umbundu of Life before and after Portuguese Colonial Rule', *Africa*, 91.5 (2021), pp. 713–41.

When Frederico initiated his fieldwork in Dakar in September 2019, he frequently heard children playfully crying
out together: 'Toubab, toubab, toubab!' as they pointed
their fingers at him. Adults were usually more discreet and
merely pointed at him.[5] He initially thought that they were
referring to Touba, the sacred city of the *muridiyya* brotherhood he used to attend during his fieldwork in Brazil. With
time, he noticed that although he used to wear a *were
wolof*, typical Senegalese clothing that had been given to
him by his friends, his phenotype (skin colour and type of
hair) and his bodily stance (the way in which he walked,
laughed, and spoke with a Brazilian accent) informed his
interlocutors that he was a *toubab* and summoned the local
codes through which his positionality was read. Generally
speaking, *toubab* refers to a person whose skin is white and
whose status is that of a foreigner of high social standing
and Western origin (coming especially from countries in
Europe and North America). Moreover, it references the
French colonial history of the country, in the context of
which local populations were racialized and an opposition
between the colonizer and the colonized was forged.[6] Yet,
a black Senegalese person can also be assigned that name
by Senegalese people who consider that he does not fit the
local criteria of belonging.[7]

---

5   A similar situation has been described by other researchers. See Gilson
     José Rodrigues Jr, 'Em nome do reino: ações humanitárias brasileiras de
     Tuparetama (Brasil) a Dakar (Senegal)' (Doctoral Dissertation, Social
     Anthropology, Centre for Philosophy and Human Sciences, Federal
     University of Pernambuco, Recife, 2019), p. 7, and Eva Evers Rosander,
     In Pursuit of Paradise: Senegalese Women, Muridism and Migration (Los
     Angeles: Nordic Africa Institute, 2015), p. 32.

6   Hélène Quashie, 'La Blanchité au miroir de l'africanité: migrations
     et constructions sociales urbaines d'une assignation identitaire peu
     explorée', *Cahiers d'études africaines*, 220 (2015), pp. 760–85 (p. 763).

7   Frederico Santos dos Santos, 'Casa de tèranga: nomeações e materi-
     alidades na migração transnacional entre Senegal e Brasil' (Doctoral

Encountering a *toubab* can also cause reactions of fear. As Frederico was traveling the 560 km that separate Mboumba from Dakar with a friend, their bus broke in front of a village and they spent hours on the road waiting for it to be fixed. As children left school to go home, they ran on the road and talked to the passengers. Frederico tried to greet them, but they were afraid and showed reservations. One of the children even cried as he tried to shake hands with him. Some of them hid between the bushes to better observe him from a distance. He was reminded of Frantz Fanon, who felt dehumanized as his presence was racialized by white children who told their mothers that they were afraid of him.[8] But the situation experienced by Frederico, differently from that of Fanon, did not question his humanity. The impression he had was that those children had never seen a *toubab*. His friend explained to him that children living in the interior of the country had probably never been to a big Senegalese city such as Touba or Dakar, where they would have met a *toubab*.

Toubab, in that it designates a social position based on the relationship between Europeans and Africans, implies a division between two classes of people, rather than between two different continents: the colonizer and the colonized. This reductive opposition between colonizer and colonized underscores the totalizing character of a system of classification historically connected to Senegalese colonial history. As affirmed by Jean and John Comaroff, despite the complexities of colonial societies, such systems tend to be perceived and represented based on a dualism that solidifies the distance between those who rule

---

Dissertation, Social Anthropology, Federal University of São Carlos, São Carlos, 2022).

8   Frantz Fanon, *Black Skin, White Masks* [1952], trans. by Charles Lam Markmann (New York: Pluto Press, 1986).

and those who are ruled, white and black, European and non-European, as well as the ways in which they inhabit such positions and identifications.[9] However, such categories are neither fixed nor stable.[10] Thus, the designation of someone as *toubab* assigns this person a marker that indexes complimentary qualities (such as modernity, seriousness, and rigor) that are simultaneously opposed to racialized African stereotypes (such as laziness, superficiality, and primitivity). Yet, *toubab* is not always a complimentary designation.

Being a *toubab* can also be synonymous with acting and thinking like a Western person, which involves having no god, being driven by *xalis* (money), being absent from life in the family and community, lacking solidarity and hospitality, and embracing individualism. These characteristics are often deeply condemned in Senegalese contexts.[11] According to Edward Said,[12] such stereotypes of the 'other' rest on historical constructions based on processes of generalization, homogenization, and inferiorization. These stereotypes construct reductive images dependent on centres of authority and canons that do not take other perspectives into account. As indicated by Iracema Dulley and Lorena Muniagurria, the processes through which 'subjects are located and displaced in different contexts occur in association with the categories

---

9   John Comaroff and Jean Comaroff, *Of Revelation and Revolution: The Dialectics of Modernity on a South African Frontier* (Chicago: The University of Chicago Press, 1997), p. 25.

10   Quashie, 'La Blanchité', p. 763.

11   Bruno Riccio, 'Talkin' about Migration: Some Ethnographic Notes on the Ambivalent Representation of Migrants in Contemporary Senegal', *Stichproben — Vienna Journal of African Studies*, 8 (2005), pp. 99–118 (p. 118) <https://stichproben.univie.ac.at/fileadmin/user_upload/p_stichproben/Artikel/Nummer08/07_Riccio.pdf> [accessed 11 March 2020].

12   Edward W. Said, *Orientalism* (New York: Pantheon Books, 1978).

that designate them and assign them a social place'.[13] In processes of interpellation, it is frequently the case that categorizations are driven by the desire to establish an absolute, sovereign distinction between the colonizer and the colonized. *Toubab*, the name employed by strangers to designate Frederico during his fieldwork, gestures towards this otherness. Yet, what defines otherness is not fixed.

In the case of Frederico, the main reason for calling him a *toubab* was his bodily appearance, for in Senegal he was considered white although in his place of origin, Rio Grande do Sul, Brazil, he was considered black. Thus, people on the streets would assume that he was not Senegalese just by looking at him. Yet, he was not called *toubab* by everyone he encountered during fieldwork. As people got to know him better, they frequently commented that he practiced *teranga*, a term imperfectly translatable as generosity: He made donations and gave alms to strangers, made himself available to help his interlocutors, and participated in religious rituals despite not identifying as a Muslim. In view of the ways in which he behaved, his position as a *toubab* was displaced on many occasions. As a fluid designation, the term *toubab* can perform either the inclusion or the exclusion of someone in the local dynamics. As he spent time with his interlocutors in their *keur* (in Wolof, both the home and the communal practices and bonds associated with it), he was assigned a social place that distanced him from that of the *toubab*.

However, his name in Portuguese, Frederico, and his usual nickname, Fred, reinforced his placement as a *toubab*, that is, as someone who does not belong to the *keur*. This

---

13   Iracema Dulley and Lorena de Avelar Muniagurria, 'Performance, processos de diferenciação e constituição de sujeitos', *R@U*, 12.1 (2020), pp. 8–18 (p. 9).

was the case until at a certain *keur* in the city of Touba, where he was given a room for the second time, the woman in charge found it difficult to pronounce his name. While the whole family was watching television after dinner, she offered him watermelon and told him that he would be called Bamba Fall from that day on. He was then offered an explanation for their choice of this name, which revealed their motivations underlying this act of naming. Bamba Fall is composed of two names: Whereas Bamba refers to Amadou Bamba, the founder of the Muslim brotherhood *muridiyya* to which the family belongs, Fall is the surname that identifies the family. Thus, upon receiving this name, Frederico was included in the family as an honorary member. They asked him to use the names Frederico and Fred only in Brazil. *Nga tudd?*, 'What is your name?', was a question he was asked by his hosts on that evening and on subsequent days. Whenever he answered Frederico or Fred, he was humorously told off. *Maa ngi tudd Bamba*, 'My name is Bamba', in turn, made everyone smile, hug him, and go with him for walks in the city. Through this act of naming, he was placed in a different position that opened new possibilities of relation and experience while also making clear what the expectations of his hosts were.

What is the relationship between Bamba Fall, the name given to Frederico, and Amadou Bamba? Although philosophical discourse frequently assumes that proper names are marks devoid of meaning, ethnographic research shows us that this is not the case at all.[14] Rather, proper names position people in the web of relations in which they operate. They connect them to certain people (as happens, for instance, in the case of surnames, in which

---

14   João de Pina-Cabral, 'Outros nomes, histórias cruzadas: apresentando o debate', *Etnográfica*, 12.1 (2008), pp. 5–16.

one's line of continuity with one's family is marked) and
differentiate them from other people (for instance, if one is
assigned an Arabic name one's belonging to a Muslim community is marked and this differentiates one from those
not encompassed by it). The distribution of proper names
among a given population does not happen randomly, for
proper names do not merely fulfil the function of des-
ignating individuals in social interactions. Instead, they
constitute a 'safe index of the socially significant character of naming practices'.[15] As Frederico was called Bamba
Fall, this did not merely create a Bamba, but a Bamba Fred.
Bamba became his name and he learned to respond to it
in mutuality. As an added layer of nomination, this name
bestowed upon him a new social position.

Naming indicates and establishes a subject in space
and time, and thus sediments this subject's positionality
in relation to others.[16] As Frederico was displaced from
the position of *toubab* through the performative act of his
naming as Bamba Fall, this inaugurated for him a different
positionality in the *keur* of his hosts and extended this new
position beyond it to the different sets of relations that
had the *keur* as their starting point. As happened with the
transliteration of the name Iracema as Iracelma, this new
name situated him in the relational context of his fieldwork.
Placed in a kind of relation with the *keur* that integrated
him as a fictive relative on the basis of *teranga*,[17] the more

15   Robert Rowland, 'Práticas de nomeação em Portugal durante a Época
      moderna — ensaio de aproximação', *Etnográfica*, 12.1 (2008), pp. 17–43.

16   On this matter, see Judith Butler, *Excitable Speech: A Politics of the Per-
      formative* (New York: Routledge, 1997), p. 33 and *An Anthropology of
      Names and Naming*, ed. by Gabriele vom Bruck and Barbara Bodenhorn
      (Cambridge: Cambridge University Press, 2009).

17   Ivy Mills, 'Sutura: Gendered Honor, Social Death and the Politics of
      Exposure in Senegalese Literature and Popular Culture' (Doctoral Dis-
      sertation, African American Studies, University of California, Berkeley,
      2011), p. 1.

Frederico approached the position of a relative, the more he distanced himself from the social place of the unrelated *toubab* and gave in to the demands of his hosts.

CONCLUDING REMARKS

What if Frederico or Iracema were to reject the names they were given and claim their social position as researchers instead? This is to be understood as a merely rhetorical question, for although anthropological research is frequently marked by a certain degree of extraction, it is also the case that anthropologists in the field are far from occupying the position of a sovereign subject. For instance, structural factors, such as funding for producing research on people historically considered 'others' in colonial and imperialist contexts, constrain as much as enable the researcher. From this perspective, the names one is given during fieldwork expose the anthropologist's vulnerability and reiterate the need to respond to the positionalities defined by one's interlocutors. As argued by Judith Butler, the subject's constitution in language can occur without her knowledge, as happens in the third-person address that interpellates a subject without requiring a response.[18] In order for one to act as a subject and not simply occupy the third-person position, one needs to respond to the names one is called.

Interpellation is not a descriptive act, about which one can determine whether it is true or false by comparing it with facts in the world. It does not have description as its main function, even though it might appear as descriptive in the context of colonial classification, ethnographic writing, or post-colonial self-presentation. Rather, interpellation establishes 'a subject in subjection, to produce

---

18   Butler, *Excitable Speech*, p. 33.

its social contours in space and time. Its reiterative operation has the effect of sedimenting its "positionality" over
time'.[19] Thus, the names given to Frederico and Iracema
by their interlocutors not only allowed them to conduct
research; the names were assigned in view of their interlocutors' appreciation of the positionalities that Frederico
and Iracema were deemed able to occupy. These names
also determined, for instance, who Iracema was going to
talk to and in what capacity and from what position of
belonging Frederico would be allowed to interact with
Senegalese families. Through acts of naming, anthropologists are placed and displaced.

People are assigned names by others everywhere, beginning with the context in which they are born and named
by their relatives. The names one receives precede and exceed oneself.[20] Yet, they do not precede and exceed one
in the same way in every situation. Based on a comparison
between Angola and Senegal, this brief position paper invites us to think through the implications of acts of naming
in different contexts. We contend that the theorization of
naming cannot depend solely on abstractions that, while
deemed universal, are in fact the result of the singular
placement of (frequently Western, male, and white) philosophers — and intersectionality studies are a powerful
tool to make this visible. Rather, generalization is always
provisional and contextual, dependent on the consideration of singular forms of nomination to be understood in
relation to the contexts and languages in which they occur.
Taking into account the relevance of social positionality
made visible by intersectionality studies, we ask: What

---

19   Butler, *Excitable Speech*, p. 34.
20   Jacques Derrida, 'Des tours de Babel', trans. by Joseph F. Graham, in
      Difference in Translation, ed. by Joseph Graham (Ithaca, NY: Cornell
      University Press, 1985), pp. 165–207.

does the constatation that proper names are not merely neutral designators of individuals in social interaction do to the theorization of naming? How can one extend general categorizations by taking into consideration other conceptualizations of it? Let us provisionally end here with this open question.

Marx on the Periphery

The Making of a New Tradition at the University of São Paulo

BERNARDO BIANCHI

> We were, however, not to Europe as
> feudalism was to capitalism; to the
> contrary, in addition to never having
> been 'feudal', we were a function of
> European capitalism on every front
>
> Roberto Schwarz, *To
> the Victor, the Potatoes!*[1]

While the Global South has come to be considered as the perfect epitome of postcolonial and decolonial studies, the concept of periphery has also played an important role that cannot be overlooked.[2] Accordingly, this 'outdated

---

1   Roberto Schwarz, *To the Victor, the Potatoes!: Literary Form and Social Process in the Beginnings of the Brazilian Novel*, ed. and trans. by Ronald W. Sousa (Leiden: Brill, 2019), p. 5.

2   For a discussion about the predominance of the term 'Global South' in contemporary analyses, cf. Caroline Levander and Walter Mignolo, 'Introduction: The Global South and World Dis/Order', *The Global South*, 5.1 (2011), pp. 1–11 <https://doi.org/10.2979/globalsouth.5.1.1>.

concept' should be viewed in light of a rich process of self-reflection undertaken by social scientists living in societies outside Europe and North America. Perhaps even more directly than the concept of the Global South, the concept of periphery conveys a spatial grasp of an unequal system, as well as of the processes of extraction and violence that underpin it. After all, it was forged in direct opposition to the temporal dualisms that rely on a teleological and stadialist conception of the variations of societies around the world, which gave rise to pairs such as civilized/savage, modern/backward, and developed/underdeveloped.

The aim of this chapter is to discuss, by means of the concept of periphery, the making of a new tradition in the social sciences in Brazil that accounts for a specific moment in the history of postcolonial and decolonial studies. Accordingly, I will begin by reviewing the innovations behind the conception of the two Marx Seminars that took place at the University of São Paulo between the late 1950s and early 1960s, which, in a unique and innovative way, reframed theoretical problems that were at the forefront of international debate. The international relevance of these experiments will lead us to discuss a contemporary endeavour, notoriously led by Louis Althusser at the École Normale Supérieure (ENS) in Rue d'Ulm, which resulted in the book *Lire Le Capital* (*Reading Capital*) in 1965.[3] In a second moment, I will analyse how the concept of periphery responds to the interpretative limitations related to the idea of backwardness that dominated Brazilian social sciences in general and Marxist reflections in particular. In this sense, the concept of periphery, as it will be discussed, is a forceful response to temporal dualisms and stadialist

---

3   Louis Althusser and others, *Reading Capital*, trans. by Ben Brewster and David Fernbach (London: Verso, 2015).

interpretations of Brazil and Latin America. Finally, by means of his interpretation of the work of Machado de Assis, I will address the literary criticism developed by Roberto Schwarz as an unavoidable chapter for understanding the centrality of the concept of periphery in this Brazilian tradition of the social sciences.

READING MARX IN SÃO PAULO

In 1958, after returning from an academic stay in France, the philosopher José Arthur Giannotti gathered friends and colleagues from the University of São Paulo (USP) to read and discuss Karl Marx's *Das Kapital*.[4] The group included the economist Paul Singer, the sociologists Octavio Ianni and Fernando Henrique Cardoso, the anthropologist Ruth Cardoso, and the historian Fernando Novais. They were joined by other frequent participants, including Roberto Schwarz, Michael Löwy, and Bento Prado Júnior.[5] Although the meetings focused on the reading of *Capital*, they also discussed other works, such as Jean-Paul Sartre's *Questions de méthode* (*Search for a Method*), published in 1957, and György Lukács's *Geschichte und Klassenbewußtsein* (*History and Class Consciousness*), the French trans-

---

4   The most important reference here is the first volume of *Capital*, published in 1867 — cf. Karl Marx, *Capital: A Critique of Political Economy, Vol I: The Process of Production of Capital*, ed. by Friedrich Engels, trans. by Samuel Moore and Edward Aveling, in *Marx and Engels Collected Works*, 50 vols (London: Lawrence & Wishart, 1975–2004), xxxv (1996).

5   Unfortunately, I do not have the space to analyse each of these authors in detail. I will limit myself to highlighting the intellectual and political importance of these participants in Brazil and Latin America, reinforced by the centrality of the University of São Paulo in this context. It should be added, however, that Fernando Henrique Cardoso was the president of Brazil from 1995 to 2002.

lation of which was published in 1960.[6] The reading of Lukács's *magnum opus*, in particular, was to have a strong influence on Schwarz, Novais, and others, be it for its role in the renewal of the European Marxist tradition, or for the centrality of questions of method.[7] In 1964, however, the group disbanded.

A few years after the founding of the first group, on the eve of the *coup d'état* that established the Brazilian military dictatorship (1964–84), a new Marx Seminar was organized in 1963. *Seminaristas* of the first group, such as Prado Júnior, Singer, Löwy, and Schwarz, participated in the new project.[8] However, other participants joined them: the philosophers João Quartim de Moraes, Marilena Chaui, and Ruy Fausto, the historian Emília Viotti, and the sociologist and philosopher Maria Sylvia de Carvalho Franco, among others.[9] Although influenced by the first seminar, including in its composition, the second one was marked by a new historical context. The *coup d'état* of April 1964 gave it a more activist character, and some of its members joined the armed resistance.[10] In any case, academic en-

---

6   Jean-Paul Sartre, *Search for a Method*, trans. by Hazel Barnes (New York: Alfred A. Knopf, 1963); György Lukács, *History and Class Consciousness: Studies in Marxist Dialectics*, trans. by Rodney Livingstone (Cambridge, MA: MIT Press, 1971).

7   The centrality of questions of method corresponds to the intention, shared by the members of the group, to defend the scientific value of Marxism in accordance with academic conventions. Cf. Paulo Arantes, *Um departamento francês de ultramar* (Rio de Janeiro: Paz e Terra, 1994), p. 43.

8   Henceforth, *Seminaristas* is the term by which I will refer to the participants of the seminars in question.

9   Cf. Roberto Schwarz, 'Sobre a leitura de Marx no Brasil', in *Nós que amávamos tanto 'O Capital'*, ed. by Emir Sader et al. (São Paulo: Boitempo, 2017), para. 1–17 (para. 4).

10   Historian Lidiane Rodrigues convincingly links the greater presence of women in the second seminar to the development of a more political orientation from the outset, in contrast to the more masculine and aca-

gagement remained intense, culminating in the creation of the journal *Teoria e Prática* (*Theory and Practice*), a publication that was interrupted in 1968 with the consolidation of the military regime.

FRENCH EXCHANGES

Almost exactly in parallel with the Marx Seminars at USP, Louis Althusser organized a seminar at ENS between 1964 and 1965. It was dedicated to the reading of *Capital*, from which, in November 1965, came the book *Lire Le Capital*, one of the most influential works in the renewal of Marxist studies in the mid-twentieth century. Although they were not linked, the USP and ENS seminars should be seen in light of the important historical circumstances that bring the two experiences together.

Firstly, the French influence in Brazil was enormous, both because of a long French-speaking tradition dating back to colonial times and, in the case of USP, because of the central role played by the French missions in its institutionalization throughout the first decades of its existence.[11] The situation was no different in the philosophy department, where many of the participants in the two Marx seminars came from. It is for this reason that Paulo Arantes dubbed the philosophy department of USP *Um departamento francês de ultramar* (*A French Overseas Department*) in his homonymous work on the formation of that academic environment. In a letter of 1957 to João Cruz

---

demic character of the first seminar. Cf. Lidiane Rodrigues, 'A produção social do marxismo universitário em São Paulo: mestres, discípulos e "um seminário" (1958–1978)' (Doctoral Dissertation, University of São Paulo, 2011), p. 46.

11 On the subject, cf. Ian Merkel, *Terms of Exchange: Brazilian Intellectuals and the French Social Sciences* (Chicago: The University of Chicago Press, 2022).

Costa, his doctoral supervisor, Giannotti wrote: 'I have adopted a motto: study modern Germans in the French fashion.'[12] Giannotti's words, which had in view the study of Marx, testify to the extent of the French influence on his project of reading the German author directly.

Secondly, both the first Marx Seminar and its French counterpart were animated by an effort to renew Marxist studies by returning to Marx's own texts, and to *Capital* in particular. But their affinities did not stop there in the eyes of Gerard Lebrun, who worked in the philosophy department of USP for six years, during which time he also attended meetings of the Marx Seminar. In 1966, he wrote on the dust jacket of *Origens da dialética do trabalho* (*Origins of the Dialectics of Labour*), by Giannotti: 'in France as in Brazil one agrees to study Marx in the way that Gueroult comments on Descartes.'[13] In fact, in 1960, in a text on the reading method used in the Seminar, Giannotti highlighted the importance of the 'structural analysis' of *Capital*.[14] This hermeneutic proposal was in line with the method of structural reading of philosophical texts that had been widely disseminated at USP by Jean Maugé, Victor Goldschmidt, and Martial Gueroult.[15] It should be remembered

---

12   Cf. Rodrigues, *A produção*, p. 34.

13   José Arthur Giannotti, *Origens da dialética do trabalho: estudo sobre lógica do jovem Marx* (São Paulo: Difel, 1966). In the same text, Lebrun also draws a parallel between Giannotti's book and *Pour Marx*, published by Althusser the previous year, affirming that both were the best books published on the German author at the time. Cf. Louis Althusser, *For Marx*, trans. by Ben Brewster (London: Verso, 2005).

14   José Arthur Giannotti, 'Notas para uma análise metodológica de "O Capital"', *Revista Brasiliense*, 29 (1960), pp. 60–72 (p. 63).

15   On Gueroult's influence on the philosophy department at USP, including the Marx Seminar, cf. Elsa Costa, '"But I Want the Truth!" The Legacy of Martial Gueroult in São Paulo Philosophy, 1935–2018', *A Contracorriente: Una revista de estudios latinoamericanos*, 18.3 (2021), pp. 70–105.

that in 1953 Gueroult published his work on Descartes, revealing his structural method of reading 'according to the order of reasons', which was widely discussed at USP.[16] However, the influence of Gueroult's structural method on Althusser's symptomatic reading cannot be argued without mediations, that is, without considering other thinkers and ideas with which Althusser openly engaged.[17] For Althusser, quite explicitly in connection with Lacan, the question required doing 'more than a mere literal reading' in order to critically grasp the structure of the problematic, that is, what a text inadvertently determines as visible and invisible.[18]

Despite the rapprochement suggested by Lebrun, Giannotti was rather critical of Althusser and the general project of *Lire Le Capital*. In 1968, in a text originally published in *Teoria e Prática*, he accused Althusser of establishing an excessively rigid separation between object of knowledge and real object.[19] The argument was revisited a few years later in an interview in which Giannotti rejected Althusser's 'epistemological standpoint that makes Marxism a theory of knowledge' in favour of 'Lukács's problematic of an ontology of the social'.[20] The critique conquered the hearts of his fellow students at the Marx Seminar, such as F. H. Cardoso, 'blocking the

---

16 Cf. Martial Gueroult, *Descartes selon l'ordre des raisons*, 2 vols (Paris: Aubier-Montaigne, 1953).

17 In fact, one could argue that Althusser and Gueroult fought against the same enemies, such as existentialist methods and humanism, embodied by Roger Garaudy (for Althusser) and Ferdinand Alquié (for Gueroult).

18 Althusser, *Reading Capital*, pp. 24 and 218.

19 Cf. José Arthur Giannotti, 'Contra Althusser', in *Exercícios de filosofia* (Petrópolis: Vozes, 1980), pp. 85–102.

20 José Arthur Giannotti, 'Entrevista com José Arthur Giannotti', *Trans/Form/Ação*, 1 (1974), pp. 25–36 (p. 36).

path of Althusserianism among us', in Arantes's words.[21]
Giannotti's critique points to an additional difference
between the two proposals: the place they assign to the
Hegelian legacy. Although Hegelian categories were
praised by Giannotti and the other *Seminaristas*, they
were, as is well known, passionately opposed by the
French philosopher and his students. In light of these
disputes, Lebrun's words may seem extravagant, but
they suggest important lines of convergence between
two experiments in the history of Marxism, without
assimilating them into each other. Faced with a common
set of historical problems, and independently from any
mutual influence, they arrived at positions that are more
similar than has been acknowledged.[22] Indeed, making
these affinities more accessible could contribute to the
deprovincialization of Marxism.

DEPROVINCIALIZING MARXISM

Unlike its French counterpart, the main objective of the
first seminar was not only to participate in the renewal
of Marxism, but also to inaugurate a discussion on Marx
within Brazilian academia, something that had already hap-

---

21   Arantes, *Um departamento francês de ultramar*, p. 291. Cf. Fernando
     Henrique Cardoso, *Política e desenvolvimento em sociedades dependen-
     tes: ideologias do empresariado industrial argentino e brasileiro* (Rio de
     Janeiro: Zahar, 1971), p. 111; Fernando Henrique Cardoso, 'Prefácio à
     2ª edição', in *Capitalismo e escravidão no Brasil meridional*, 5th edn (Rio
     de Janeiro: Civilização Brasileira, 2003), pp. 15–24 (pp. 20–24). Cf.
     also Pedro Lima, 'As desventuras do Marxismo: Fernando Henrique
     Cardoso, antagonismo e reconciliação (1955–1968)' (Doctoral Disser-
     tation, Universidade do Estado do Rio de Janeiro, 2015).

22   One common ground is precisely the critique of temporal dualism,
     which will occupy the following section. I do not have the space to
     analyse Althusser's approach to the problem, but I would like to draw
     attention to his critique of the concept of feudalism in his writings on
     Montesquieu. Cf. Louis Althusser, *Montesquieu: la politique et l'histoire*
     (Paris: PUF, 1992).

pened in France. In appropriating Marx, the *Seminaristas* also sought to answer why Marx was relatively absent from the Brazilian academic debate. That is, why was Marxism not a real instrument for the self-understanding of the Brazilian reality within the universities? The answer lay in the history of Marxism in Brazil (and Latin America), given the limitations of this tradition to interpret this particular social reality. The Marx Seminar is still remembered more for the way in which it changed how Brazilians understand their society than for the renewal of Marxism itself. Against the obsolete temporal dualisms inherent in the Marxist tradition that, with rare exceptions, prevailed during the Stalinist period, it was urgent to reinvent theoretical approaches to colonialism and slavery. In doing so, the members of both seminars converged in a 'single critical environment', as Schwarz stated in relation to the work of two *Seminaristas*, about whom I will speak more below.[23]

During the Stalinist period, Latin American communist parties defended a predominantly 'provincial' position for the subcontinent that was structured by a stadialist ideology, that is, a dogmatic view based on a temporal dualism.[24] This ideology, directly promoted by the Soviet Union, presupposed the need for a revolution in two stages. Firstly, there would be a national bourgeois revolution of democratic character against the local oligarchies. Secondly, the development and maturation of the productive

---

23   Roberto Schwarz, 'Um seminário de Marx', in *Sequências brasileiras: ensaios* (São Paulo: Companhia das Letras, 1999), pp. 86–105 (p. 97).

24   It is worth noting that an analogous question began to generate controversy among researchers involved in the project led by Althusser, namely the relationship of the French Communist Party (PCF) to the Algerian war. In 1981, Balibar was expelled from the PCF precisely because of his criticism of that party's orthodox and colonialist position on Algeria. Cf. Don Reid, 'Etienne Balibar: Algeria, Althusser, and Altereuropéenisation', *South Central Review*, 25.3 (2008), pp. 68–85.

forces (there was little distinction between objective and subjective conditions of revolutionary processes) would lead to an actual socialist revolution. The debates associated with the Brazilian Communist Party (PCB) reproduced this dominant dualist ideology. The resulting attempts to interpret Brazil, from Astrojildo Pereira to Nelson Werneck Sodré, relied on a reading of Brazilian society from a predominantly stadialist perspective that constantly revolved around the concepts of backwardness and feudalism.[25]

Trapped in this interpretation, such analyses understood backwardness only negatively — in terms of 'lack' or 'deficit' — and not positively — in terms of how it is actually constituted, namely, as a result of the unique historical development of a country and the role a country plays within the global economy. Thus, the explanation in terms of backwardness became a story about how oligarchic greed and popular immobility combined to form a single essentialized block that could only be broken by an alliance between the most modern elements of society. Against this perspective, the *Seminaristas* have urged for backwardness to be seen not as a vestige of the past, but as the present realization of a subaltern role.[26] Brazil and Latin America were

---

25   For Pereira's main texts, cf. Astrojildo Pereira, *Ensaios históricos e políticos*, ed. by Heitor Ferreira Lima (São Paulo: Alfa-Omega, 1979). The reference to a 'semi-feudalism' is recurrent. Nelson Werneck Sodré has given more systematic treatment to the notion of feudalism, which he expounded throughout his vast work. Cf. Nelson Werneck Sodré, *Capitalismo e revolução burguesa no Brasil* (Belo Horizonte: Nossa Terra, 1990).

26   It is important to note that similar responses to this problem have emerged from quite different contexts. Therefore, it is worth mentioning Raúl Prebisch's research in the context of CEPAL or ECLAC (United Nations Economic Commission for Latin America and the Caribbean) and, among the contributors to the *Monthly Review*, the works of André Gunder Frank, who later became one of the founders of dependency theory. Cf. Raúl Prebisch, 'The Economic Development of

never feudal, just as they were never pre-capitalist. According to Schwarz, the great novelty that emerged from the seminars was the investigation of the 'effective connections between capitalism and slavery', thus breaking with the formalist perspective according to which slavery was the other of capitalism.[27] These innovations crystallized in two seminal works written by *Seminaristas* from the two groups: *Capitalismo e escravidão no Brasil meridional* (*Capitalism and Slavery in Southern Brazil*), by Fernando Henrique Cardoso, and *Homens livres na ordem escravocrata* (*Free Men in the Slave Order*), by Maria Sylvia de Carvalho Franco.[28] In addition, there is the doctoral dissertation of Fernando Novais, which, although defended in 1973, deals with the same set of questions that I am addressing here. Moreover, Novais, like Schwarz and Cardoso, concedes an important role to Caio Prado Júnior in his work. [29]

Latin America and Its Principal Problems', Economic Commission for Latin America, 1950 <https://repositorio.cepal.org/handle/11362/29973> [accessed 11 February 2023]; Andre Gunder Frank, *Capitalism and Underdevelopment in Latin America: Historical Studies of Chile and Brazil* (New York: Monthly Review Press, 1967).

27   Cf. Schwarz, 'Um seminário de Marx', p. 93. Of course, this innovation has to be put into perspective, given the existence of notable works that have followed similar paths. I refer to *Black Jacobins* (1938), by C. L. R. James, and *Formação do Brasil contemporâneo* (*Formation of Contemporary Brazil*) (1942), by Caio Prado Júnior, a dissenting voice within the PCB. Cf. C. L. R. James, *The Black Jacobins: Toussaint L'Ouverture and the San Domingo Revolution* (New York: Penguin, 2001); Caio Prado Jr, *Formação do Brasil contemporâneo* (São Paulo: Companhia das Letras, 2011).

28   Both works are the result of doctoral dissertations. Cardoso's was defended in 1961 and published in 1962. Cf. Fernando Henrique Cardoso, *Capitalismo e escravidão no Brasil meridional: o negro na sociedade escravocrata do Rio Grande do Sul*, 5th edn (Rio de Janeiro: Civilização Brasileira, 2003). Carvalho Franco's thesis was defended in 1964 but not published until 1969. Cf. Maria Sylvia de Carvalho Franco, *Homens livres na ordem escravocrata*, 4th edn (São Paulo: UNESP, 1983).

29   Cf. Fernando Novais, *Portugal e Brasil na crise do antigo sistema colonial (1777–1808)*, 5th edn (São Paulo: Hucitec, 1989).

CONCLUSION: SCHWARZ AND MACHADO DE ASSIS

Against this background, I mark the historical and theoretical significance of Schwarz's contribution. Years after the end of the seminars, but still under the influence of their 'critical environment', Schwarz published an article in 1973 entitled *As ideias fora do lugar* (*Misplaced Ideas*).[30] This text already reveals Schwarz's deep interest in the late-nineteenth-century Brazilian writer Joaquim Maria Machado de Assis, a reverence he later developed in his own doctoral dissertation, *To the Victor, the Potatoes!*, and *A Master on the Periphery of Capitalism*.[31] Through Machado de Assis's novels, Schwarz delves into the Brazilian reality of the time not to reveal its singularity, but to show that the texture of this society is produced in interaction with a world economic system. Schwarz's texts on Machado de Assis thus disclose important resonances with the work of other *Seminaristas*, whether in exploring the links between free and slave labour or in valorizing the standpoint of totality.

For Schwarz, the world described by Machado de Assis represents the very denial of the stadialist ideology as a valid interpretative key for nineteenth-century Brazilian society. Moreover, Schwarz's analyses of Machado de Assis are much more in line with what Fredric Jameson called 'spatial dialectic'.[32] Accordingly, what is disclosed is not

---

30   Roberto Schwarz, 'As Ideias fora do lugar', in *Ao Vencedor as Batatas* (São Paulo: Editora 34, 2000), p. 17.

31   Schwarz, *To the Victor*; Roberto Schwarz, *A Master on the Periphery of Capitalism: Machado de Assis*, trans. by John Gledson, Post-Contemporary Interventions (Durham, NC: Duke University Press, 2001).

32   Fredric Jameson, *Valences of the Dialectic* (London: Verso Books, 2010), pp. 66–70. This point has been convincingly argued by Nicholas Brown. Cf. Nicholas Brown, 'Roberto Schwarz: Mimesis Beyond Realism', in *The SAGE Handbook of Frankfurt School Critical Theory*,

merely 'national in scope, but reaches out to the dynamic of what an older vocabulary called "combined and uneven development", the differential development of capitalism across geographic and political space'.[33] In the first place, then, the concept of periphery marks a preference for the spatial, the geographical, at the expense of the stadial and teleological, which are rooted in the temporal dualisms discussed here.

The concept of periphery is thus articulated from a critique of the conception of backwardness insofar as the latter presupposes an endogenous and diachronic conception of national development. The periphery, in turn, describes a situation of dependence in relation to a centre or core that produces an international space stratified by the unequal distribution of wealth, values, and knowledge. In this very process, the centre imposes itself as the universal model of civilization, the *telos* of human development. In this sense, however, it becomes clear that the concept of periphery explains the idea of backwardness, but the latter can never account for the former, just as it cannot explain the social processes that produce it.

---

ed. by Beverley Best, Werner Bonefeld, and Chris O'Kane, 3 vols (Los Angeles: SAGE, 2018), I, pp. 465–78 (p. 471). It should be noted, however, that the description that Schwarz analyses as *dialectical*, as opposed to dualist ideologies, has been famously defended by Paulo Arantes. Cf. Paulo Arantes, *Sentimento da dialética na experiência intelectual brasileira. Dialética e dualidade segundo Antonio Cândido e Roberto Schwarz* (São Paulo: Paz e Terra, 1992).

33   Brown, 'Roberto Schwarz', p. 471.

Inner World and Milieu
Art, Madness, and Brazilian Psychiatry in the Work of Nise da Silveira

MARLON MIGUEL

INTRODUCTION

In the recent renewed interest for historical instances of alternative and 'radical psychiatries',[1] Global South figures are systematically missing. The Brazilian Psychiatric Reform, for instance, which developed very interesting strategies of care and established direct dialogues with Anti-Psychiatry movements, psychoanalysis, Italian Democratic Psychiatry, and Institutional Psychotherapy, is hardly discussed outside of Brazil. The psychiatrist

*   I would like to thank the Museum of Images from the Unconscious for granting me access to their archives, as well as the right to reproduce the images used here.

1   See for example Camille Robcis, *Disalienation: Politics, Philosophy, and Radical Psychiatry in Postwar France* (Chicago: The University of Chicago Press, 2021).

125

Nise da Silveira, who anticipated many elements of this Reform — in particular with her critique of closed and segregationist structures, as well as of hyper-diagnostication and medicalization — is one of the figures who are completely overlooked by European and Anglophone academia. Nise can be considered an iconoclast who engaged with several European psychiatrists, psychoanalysts, and thinkers to produce a very innovative reflection and practical clinical work using artistic expression to treat psychiatric patients, especially those diagnosed as psychotic.[2] As I will demonstrate in this chapter, her work strikingly engages with and unsettles established European theoretical frameworks at once. Despite being a pioneer in her field and a relatively well-known public figure in Brazil, her work has been completely overlooked abroad — and, even in Brazil, remains understudied.

There are a couple of reasons why her work has not received the attention it merits. Despite having published many texts and books, she remained above all a practitioner who never systematized her speculations. Because of her non-orthodoxy, she never belonged to any school of thought and always referred freely and eclectically, often even loosely, to thinkers such as Spinoza, Antonin Artaud, and Carl Gustav Jung, who were nonetheless crucial to her theoretical-practical developments. Moreover, her assumed affiliation with Jung rather than with Sigmund Freud or Jacques Lacan, as well as her interest in themes considered polemical — such as mandalas, archetypes, or the collective unconscious — are also factors that have

---

2   One often refers to public persons in Brazilian Portuguese using their first name instead of their family name. I will thus refer to her in this way throughout this essay. Many who were close to the psychiatrist would also call her '*Doutora* Nise' (Doctor Nise) as a term of endearment.

contributed to her 'minorization'. Finally, although Nise was relatively recognized in the Brazilian public sphere, she remained an isolated figure. Such isolation was determined both by her marginal social position — that of a woman coming from the northeast of Brazil, practicing within a deeply masculine and patriarchal environment in Rio de Janeiro — and by her methods — her work was associated with art therapy rather than with a so-called 'true' clinical method.

In this essay, I propose a double movement. On the one hand, I address Nise's work and how she produced a very innovative and situated reflection on and practice with psychosis through her non-orthodox engagement with European traditions. In particular, I focus on her critical engagement with psychoanalysis and her resonances with the French Institutional Psychotherapy movement, of which she was a direct contemporary. On the other hand, I propose to tackle the obfuscation of her work within and beyond Brazil, which can be partly explained by the fact that she was a Global South practitioner speaking from and to the South despite her far-reaching work on the visibility of the question of madness.

ART AND MADNESS IN BRAZIL

In order to grasp the historical significance of Nise's pioneering work, it is crucial to inscribe her practice in the Brazilian context of both modern art and psychiatry. Interestingly, they are intimately connected.

In the 1920s in Brazil, the reorganization of psychiatric institutions took place simultaneously with the beginning of the Brazilian modernist movement. Freud is, for example, a key figure of Oswald de Andrade's *Manifesto*

Antropófago (1928),[3] but also for artists such as Tarsila do Amaral and Flávio de Carvalho. In 1933, the latter organized with Osório César, psychiatrist and author of the seminal book *The Artistic Expression of the Alienated* (1929),[4] the famous exhibition *O Mês das Crianças e dos Loucos* (*The Month of Children and the Mad*). Carvalho claimed on that occasion that 'the only art is abnormal art'.[5] This statement can be seen as a sort of critical reversal if one considers that, in the European context, national-socialism and fascism disseminated precisely at this moment the *entartete Kunst* (degenerate art) discourse. Moreover, more than just a provocation, it also reveals a particularity of the Brazilian context in that the institutionalization of modern art is inseparable from the production of the so-called 'mad people' (*loucos*).[6] An indicator thereof is the fact that one of the first exhibitions of the São Paulo Modern Art Museum, which opened in 1947, was an exhibition made up exclusively of works by psychiatric patients from the Juquery Hospital.

However, except for the very few more progressive experimentations, such as those conducted at Juquery, the

---

3   Oswald de Andrade, 'Cannibalist Manifesto', trans. by Leslie Bary, *Latin American Literary Review*, 19.38 (1991), pp. 38–47 <https://www.jstor.org/stable/20119601>.

4   His book was a contemporary of other works on this subject, such as: Walter Morgenthaler, *Ein Geisteskranker als Künstler: Adolf Wölfli* [1921] (Bern: Zentrum Paul Klee, 2021); Hans Prinzhorn, *Bildnerei der Geisteskranken* [1922] (Hamburg: Severus Verlag, 2016); Jean Vinchon, *L'Art et la folie* (Paris: Stock, 1924).

5   Flávio de Carvalho, 'A única arte que presta é a arte anormal', in *Diário de S. Paulo* (24 September 1936), Documents of Latin American and Latino Art, International Center for the Arts of the Americas, Museum of Fine Arts, Houston <https://icaa.mfah.org/s/en/item/1084943> [accessed 20 September 2023].

6   See Kaira Cabañas, *Learning from Madness: Brazilian Modernism and Global Contemporary Art* (Chicago: The University of Chicago Press, 2018).

Brazilian psychiatric system remains extremely racist and reactionary. It can even be considered an instrument of social regulation that rejects certain parts of the population, in particular of Afro-descendants.[7] Foucault has described how certain statements (*énoncés*) can be typical of a certain time.[8] In this context, examples of such statements included the so-called 'pathologies of the poor' and of 'black people', which freely circulated; psychiatry is thus transformed into an apparatus to 'whiten' the population. As a consequence, black patients are usually hospitalized for a much longer period than white patients. Moreover, the teachings of Freud, the same figure who inspired the Brazilian avant-gardes, have been uncannily instrumentalized and mobilized by these psychiatric discourses in order to legitimize social Darwinism and the overdeterminism of the psyche.

RECONSIDERING THE SPACE: ANOTHER CONCEPT OF CARE

Nise da Silveira started to work as a psychiatrist in Rio de Janeiro in 1936. Shortly afterwards, however, during the Getúlio Vargas dictatorship (1937–45), she was sent to prison twice for a total of three months and was forbidden to practice until 1944. She often mentions how her carceral experience was crucial for her rethinking of psychiatry:[9]

---

7   See Joel Birman, 'O negro no discurso psiquiátrico', in *Cativeiro e liberdade*, ed. by Jaime da Silva et al. (Rio de Janeiro: UERJ, 1989), pp. 44–58; Lilia Moritz Schwarcz, *O espetáculo das raças: cientistas, instituições e questão racial no Brasil. 1870–1930* (São Paulo: Companhia das Letras, 2005), pp. 189–238.

8   Michel Foucault, *L'Archéologie du savoir* (Paris: Gallimard, 1969).

9   'Those months spent in Detention and Correction were the greatest human experience of my life. I think that every psychoanalyst should spend a year in prison.' Nise da Silveira, 'Interview with Márcio Moreira Alves for the Newspaper *Correio da Manhã* (1959)', quoted by Luiz

first, to reconsider the space of psychiatric institutions; second, to elaborate on the notion of 'activity' as a method to think through her clinical work:

> From the start, the architecture, the spaces of the psychiatric hospital show the concept of disease that we have. There were corridors and ambulatory rooms, as if it were a surgical hospital. [...] I developed an interest in therapy through activity.[10]

Coming back to a psychiatric hospital in 1946, Nise refused to make use of traditional methods such as Electroshock Therapy (ECT), insulin therapy, and lobotomy. Instead, she created the Section for Occupational Therapy, a section offering several ateliers in which patients could practice many activities, especially artistic ones. From Nise's perspective, this would be the occasion for them to re-elaborate their personal dramas and traumas. As a psychiatrist, she constantly emphasizes the importance of the space and ambiance — of the context of expressive production.

When treating and hosting patients, Nise also highlights the need of *afeto* (affect) or *afeto catalisador* (catalysing affect) and of *cuidado* (care) as notions guiding her clinical practice. In Portuguese, 'affect' also has a positive connotation, which is absent from the English word. When one talks about 'afeto', a positive and supportive attitude of acceptance and even encouragement is implied. For Nise, the cultivation of affect helps structure a 'supportive mi-

---

Carlos Mello, *Nise da Silveira. Caminhos de uma psiquiatra rebelde* (Rio de Janeiro: Automática, 2014), p. 81. All translations, unless otherwise noted, are mine.

10   Nise da Silveira, 'Nise da Silveira, Artaud e Jung', interview with David Bocai et al. for *Rádice* (1976–77), in Luiz Carlos Mello, *Encontros/Nise da Silveira* (Rio de Janeiro: Azougue, 2009), pp. 44–75 (p. 49).

lieu' that is necessary for the healing process. The word *cuidado*, in its turn, is equally crucial to the extent that it reflects its double, Latin etymological origin: it stems from both *cura* — implying an attitude of care, attention, and listening — and *cogitare* — thus also implying a degree of reflexivity.

Furthermore, in this context of the newly established Section, Nise took a stance embracing artistic activity as a legitimate clinical means to treat mental illness rather than as a mere form of distraction for the patient. According to her, such activities could act upon the subject's interiority and exteriority and establish a relationship between them during the clinical process. In her terms:

> the occupational therapy I sought to adopt was based on expressive activities that were capable of saying something about both the individual's interiority and the individual's relation to the mi-lieu.[11]

Until now, the significance of the notion of 'milieu' for Nise has been very little researched and I consider it a blind spot regarding her work's reception. In her practice, shifting away from the patient-doctor relationship towards what she calls the 'co-therapeutic' elements, which work as 'catalysts' within a given milieu, is crucial.[12] Such elements include animals, tools, objects, materials, or any person present in the space (a doctor, a nurse, a visitor). This is particularly important regarding psychotic patients, in which case the usual setting of the one-to-one talking cure

11   Nise da Silveira, 'O mundo contemporâneo é impaciente', interview with Luiz Carlos Lisboa, *O Estado de São Paulo,* newspaper online archive, 24 January 1987, p. 58 <https://acervo.estadao.com.br/> [accessed 1 February 2023].

12   Nise da Silveira, *Imagens do Inconsciente* (Rio de Janeiro: Alhambra, 1981), p. 69.

is often much less effective. Thus, Nise demonstrates how any aspect of a context of care may have a 'clinical function'. Indeed, I propose to think about her practice through the conception of a constructed milieu, conceived as a transferential space for the patient — or as in Jean Oury's interesting notion of 'burst transference' (*transfert éclaté*),[13] i.e., a transference not based (only) in the patient-doctor (or analyst-analysand) relationship, but mediated by these several elements dispersed in a milieu.

In this regard, it was productive for me to situate Nise's interventions through the concepts developed from the 1950s onward by the French movements, which struggled to radically rethink clinical settings. For example, I find an ally in Fernand Deligny,[14] who developed important experimental and theoretical work with autistic children, as well as in Oury and François Tosquelles,[15] who developed the principles of Institutional Psychotherapy. These encounters shifted my focus onto the notion of 'milieu' and its operationality in rethinking and restructuring clinical settings, which are also apparent in Nise's work. Indeed, Nise is a contemporary of such authors and developed her reflection and practice in parallel with them. In this sense, what I try to do here is not a projection of alien concepts onto her work. Instead, my efforts concentrate on showing

13   According to Oury, '[w]hat appears to us to be the fundamental principle of our action is the question of transference and its modalities: burst transference, "dissociated transference"'. For him, '[a]ll this shows the impossibility of psychotherapeutically taking in charge a psychotic person if one is alone and if there is no reference milieu.' See Jean Oury, 'Psychanalyse, psychiatrie et psychothérapie institutionnelles', *VST — Vie sociale et traitements*, 95 (2007), pp. 110–125 (p. 115) <https://doi.org/10.3917/vst.095.0110>.

14   See Fernand Deligny, *Camering: Fernand Deligny on Cinema and the Image*, ed. by Marlon Miguel (Leiden: LUP, 2022).

15   See François Tosquelles, *Soigner les institutions* (Paris: L'Arachnéen, 2021).

a dimension that was already there, operating in her practice, but that has not been investigated so far.

CRITIQUE OF THE PSYCHIATRIC INSTITUTION: NISE DA SILVEIRA AND FRANTZ FANON

In parallel to her work in the asylum, Nise created a space called Casa das Palmeiras (House of the Palm Trees) in 1956. She defined it as a 'free territory' with open doors where the distinctions between patients, doctors, and nurses were blurred.[16] This setting guided her elaboration of the critique of the psychiatric institution. Nise's critique consists in showing that by isolating the patient from their usual and original milieu, the hospital in fact helps to crystallize the pathology. Again, the notion of 'milieu' plays an important role in her argumentation. For instance, she claimed that

> the hospital reinforces the pathology because it does not help to re-establish the connections between the patient and their milieu, from which they were separated because of the pathology. [...] The hospital becomes an extremely efficient apparatus for the chronification of pathology.[17]

Furthermore, if the mental pathology turns the subject into a fragmented entity incapable of dealing with their usual daily milieu, Nise centres the treatment on the notion of 'activity', thanks to which the fragmented state of the ill

---

16   Nise da Silveira, *Casa das Palmeiras: a emoção de lidar, uma experiência em psiquiatria* (Rio de Janeiro: Alhambra, 1986), p. 12. The word 'territory' would later play an important role in the Brazilian Movement for the Psychiatric Reform and the project of dismantling the asylum-structures.

17   Nise da Silveira, '20 anos de Terapêutica Ocupacional em Engenho de Dentro', *Revista Brasileira de Saúde Mental*, 10 (1966), pp. 17–160 (p. 47).

subject might eventually find their unity again. Referring to Gaston Bachelard, she searches for a 'materialized psychoanalysis' in which physical work with materials may constitute a fundamental feature of working through the pathology and hallucinations;[18] in sum, the aim of a materialized psychoanalysis is to give form to the destructive emotions that dramatically submerge the patient. Here, another Portuguese word plays a key role in her argumentation: *lidar*, to deal with, to manipulate (a material), to confront. This verb also relates etymologically to *litigar*, that is, to conflict. In this sense, the patient's confrontation with certain materials could also reflect conflicts taking place within their unconscious.

My hypothesis is that the reflection developed by Nise in the context of Casa das Palmeiras is close to that of Frantz Fanon's late texts from the end of the 1950s regarding the day hospital. Though Fanon and Nise did not read each other's work, they developed strikingly similar reflections. This similarity can be partially explained by their shared references to psychoanalysis and existential psychiatry, but more important is their situatedness within peripheral and colonial conjunctures of the Global South context. They both emphasized the importance of engaging with the subject's *lived experience* so that clinical work can tackle this very context.

According to Fanon, an institution open to the outside, where the patient is no longer isolated, is the only effective way to confront 'an illness as lived by a patient, a personality in crisis within a present environment'. This is because such an illness is not 'a disorder of affectivity *in abstracto*, isolated as a symptom in a delusion or in the course of an

---

18   Gaston Bachelard, *La Terre et les rêveries du repos* (Paris: Librairie José Corti, 1982), p. 258.

interview. Instead, it is a manifest and perceptible ambivalence that tears to shreds the synthetic unity of the person and the milieu daily'.[19]

Though the Brazilian and Algerian contexts are radically different, both societies are marked by an indisputable colonial element that structures the functioning of the asylum-form. Pointing out contextual differences and similarities would demand further analysis. Yet, in both Global South contexts, the psychiatric institution plays an even more direct role in social control and alienation, which might have led both psychiatrists to arrive at similar conclusions regarding mental pathologies and their treatments. For instance, in the Algerian psychiatric sector, racist European theories were predominant, and the role the colonial war has played in the traumatic state of patients taken in charge is ignored — these elements count among the reasons that led Fanon to leave the Blida-Joinville Hospital for Tunisia at the end of 1956.[20] In Brazil, as we have seen, the situation was not very different; racist and social elements are rarely taken into account when treating patients, and the segregationist racist policy, at the base of the Brazilian system, was even intensified during the later years of military dictatorship (1964–85).[21] As Fanon points out, the catastrophic or apocalyptic 'atmosphere' of war and the colonial situation are key elements in psychosis,

19   Frantz Fanon, 'Day Hospitalization in Psychiatry: Value and Limits. Part Two: — Doctrinal Considerations', in Fanon, *Alienation and Freedom*, ed. by Jean Khalfa and Robert J. C. Young, trans. by Steven Corcoran (London: Bloomsbury, 2018), pp. 495–510 (p. 501).

20   See Frantz Fanon, 'Letter to the Resident Minister', in Fanon, *Alienation and Freedom*, pp. 433–35.

21   See Marlon Miguel, 'Psychiatric Power: Exclusion and Segregation in the Brazilian Mental Health System', in *Democracy and Brazil: Collapse and Regression*, ed. by Bernardo Bianchi et al. (London: Routledge, 2020), pp. 250–67.

although they are generally ignored by institutionalized psychiatry.[22]

In this sense, for both Fanon and Nise, there was a need for open institutional structures. Only such structures could maintain ongoing contact between the patient and society, as well as between the patient and their original milieu, strengthening the healing process and overcoming the chronification of the pathology. Furthermore, both insist on the restructuring of institutional roles and spaces within the hospital in ways that support the patient's 'activity' — Fanon speaks about the significance of the 'work scheme' in which patients invest themselves in their healing process.[23] This term resonates directly with the experience he acquired with Tosquelles in the Saint-Alban Clinic, where the Institutional Psychotherapy movement began, and where Fanon did his residency for just over a year (1952–53). In this respect, 'activity' is often considered the core of Tosquelles's method, a *clinique* of activity'.[24] Similarly, Nise thinks about the 'club' as a space for both patients and non-patients, one that cultivates collective occasions that engage every person in presence through organizing parties, poetry readings, and theatre plays.[25]

First, these collective occasions help the patients deal with their symptoms not only within the artificiality of the hospital but also closer to their existential position, which

---

22   Frantz Fanon, *The Wretched of the Earth*, trans. by Richard Philcox (New York: Grove Press, 2004).

23   Frantz Fanon, 'The Meeting between Society and Psychiatry', in Fanon, *Alienation and Freedom*, pp. 511–30 (p. 522).

24   See Yves Clot, *Éthique et travail collectif. Controverses* (Toulouse: Érès, 2020), p. 52.

25   In the context of Casa das Palmeiras, she creates the Club Caralâmpia. Tosquelles, and later Oury at La Borde and Fanon at Blida-Joinville, think the club-form as a crucial structure organized by patients inside a mental health institution.

shapes their pathology that comes to the surface within everyday life and collectivity. In such a strategy, as Fanon claims, 'there is no pointillist approach to different symptoms, but a global tackling of a form of existence, a structure, a personality engaged in current conflicts.'[26] Second, these occasions, indeed, 'activate' the suffering subject and help them actualize their tendency to heal. In this context, Nise develops a theoretical principle loosely based on her readings of Spinoza, according to which the psyche is, despite the pathology, marked by a kind of *conatus*, a tendency towards self-preservation and self-healing.[27] Nise recognizes the mandalas and circular figures painted by her patients as examples of this tendency and of a mechanism of the 'psyche's defence' against the imbalance caused by the pathology.[28] However, this tendency remains very fragile and, in order to recover it, she claims that it is necessary to move away from the excessive attention usually given to diagnoses and the symptoms of the pathology; rather, one should structure a supportive milieu that allows for the patient's affective world to be re-articulated. In cases of severe psychosis, when speech is lacking or completely disarticulated, Nise further emphasizes the need for nonverbal expressive activities such as painting.

Though they both see the observation of patients' symptoms as an essential part of the clinical work, Fanon and Nise seem to emphasize that such observation should only take place 'in action', which is to say, in the concrete situations with which the patients are engaged. As we have seen, Fanon says that the pathology is not simply a disorder but implies a 'form of existence'. Later, taking an even more

---

26 Fanon, 'Day Hospitalization', p. 502.
27 Nise da Silveira, *Cartas a Spinoza* (Rio de Janeiro: Francisco Alves, 1995), p. 81.
28 Silveira, *Imagens do Inconsciente*, p. 55.

radical stance and mobilizing Antonin Artaud, Nise will leave behind nosological conceptualizations (e.g. 'schizophrenia') to speak rather of 'dangerous states of being'.[29]

As mentioned before, Fanon and Nise did not read each other's work but arrived at similar conclusions and approaches, for instance: the importance of taking into account the lived experience (*Erlebnis*) of the subject;[30] the critique of the psychiatric institution as marked by a colonial drive of social regulation; the centrality of the patient's 'alienation' and lack of freedom caused by the mental pathology.[31] These are some points that would demand further analysis. From a theoretical perspective, such similarities could also be explained by their shared references to authors coming from a tradition related to phenomeno-

---

29   Nise da Silveira, *Os inumeráveis estados do ser* (Rio de Janeiro: Museu de Imagens do Inconsciente, 1987), p. 5

30   The question of the lived experience traverses all Fanon's writing. He refers more specifically to *Erlebnis* when commenting on Lacan's dissertation — see Frantz Fanon, 'Mental Alterations, Character Modifications, Psychic Disorders and Intellectual Deficit in Spinocerebellar Heredodegeneration: A Case of Friedreich's Ataxia with Delusions of Possession', in Fanon, *Alienation and Freedom*, pp. 203–76 (p. 264). Nise, in her turn, takes it over from Jung in relation to the importance of the '*vida vivida*' (lived life, *Erlebnis*) (Nise da Silveira, *Imagens do Inconsciente*, p. 107).

31   Fanon, following the psychiatrist Henri Ey, considers the mental disorder a 'pathology of the freedom': 'In any phenomenology in which the major alterations of consciousness are left aside, mental illness is presented as a veritable pathology of freedom. Illness situates the patient in a world in which his or her freedom, will, and desires are constantly broken by obsessions, inhibitions, countermands, and anxieties. Classical hospitalization considerably limits the patient's field of activity, prohibits all compensations, all movement, retrains him within the closed field of the hospital and condemns him to exercise his freedom in the unreal world of fantasy' (Fanon, 'Day Hospitalization', p. 497). The same Henri Ey visited Nise and the Museum of Images from the Unconscious in 1956, but there is very little information about their exchanges. In Nise's library, though, one can find Henri Ey's complete works.

logical psychiatry.[32] And these authors provide a context for understanding how both Fanon and Nise mobilize the notion of milieu and put it in relation to the inner world of the patient.

ARTISTIC EXPRESSION AS A CLINICAL MEANS

Despite the difficulties encountered inside the psychiatric hospital, Nise insists on keeping collective and creative activities going, including the circulation of people through this setting, to blur the radical division between inside and outside. The idea of creating a museum *inside* the hospital, allowing for the circulation of figures that would not otherwise go to such spaces, is, in this sense, very interesting. Nise collaborated with artists and critics — Mário Pedrosa, in particular, played a very important role there. Although her collaborators did not directly guide the patients' expressive production, they supported the creation of a setting encouraging that. For instance, they helped choose materials and tools as well as put together exhibitions. This creative context not only participates in the clinical process, but also plays a role in the political task of making the question of madness visible by animating a discursivity that accompanies the work produced by patients. In doing so, Nise confronts the double alienation reflected by the pathology: that of society and that of patients.

---

32   Beyond the several references cited throughout the text, Nise navigates through many others, such as Eugen Bleuler's observation of the transformation of the function of spatial orientation in schizophrenia. Or Eugène Minkowski's notions of 'lived space' and 'lived time', which transform, for example, the assessment of how distances between objects are experienced differently according to the existential and mental state of the subject. Her other influences include Maurice Merleau-Ponty and Ludwig Binswanger for addressing the relationship between space, affect, and one's health condition.

The starting point for Nise remains the question of how to deal with psychosis from a non-medicalized and non-violent strategy — in this sense, she differs from the methods used by Fanon and Institutional Psychotherapy. To many of her patients, the trigger of their clinical process had to be non-verbal. That is why expressive activities seemed to be a good strategy to start the work. As she claims, 'for us, the image is valid in itself, it speaks for itself, and it speaks in a loquacious way'.[33] A good example of her clinical method can be seen with a very well-known artist of Nise's Section, Fernando Diniz. According to Nise, Diniz needed to arrange and frame objects in order to organize the flow of sensations and images he violently experienced.

When Diniz was first hospitalized in 1949, it was after having been arrested by the police because he was swimming naked in Copacabana. He spent almost the rest of his life in the asylum. As a black, poor subject, Diniz was a typical target of the racist psychiatric system. He spent his childhood in the invasive atmosphere of homes shared by several people, and Nise identified his need for a place of his own. In the beginning, the space within his paintings, which were populated by overlapping objects, appears disorienting. He subsequently discovered the possibility to gradually organize this space in a series of works. First, he draws the 'baselines' of the floor; second, he draws new series of works in which the objects are separated from one another by being located in separate paintings; finally, he brings them together again in a new single work. By gradually structuring his paintings, Diniz began to 're-appropriate the daily space, he tried to recover reality'.[34]

---

33   Nise da Silveira, 'Os documentos vivos do inconsciente, a expressão plástica como forma de linguagem dos psicóticos', quoted by Mello, *Nise da Silveira. Caminhos de uma psiquiatria rebelde*, p. 139.

34   Silveira, *Imagens do Inconsciente*, p. 42.

Regarding Nise's involvement with the expressive production of patients like Diniz, it might be helpful to look at
some references that inspired her work, such as, in particular, Wilhelm Worringer and his book *Abstraktion und Ein-
fühlung* (Abstraction and Empathy).[35] According to Worringer, the cosmos inspires anguish and anxiety, and in order
to confront it, techniques of abstract painting are mobilized
by the subject, who seeks refuge and defends themself from
the invasive power exercised by surrounding objects. Alongside abstraction, Nise observes that geometrical painting
techniques are also recurrently mobilized by her patients
as a strategy for organizing chaos. Carlos Pertuis, another
important artist of the Section, at one point paints faces that
he then encloses in geometric spaces (Figure 1). This constitutes, according to Nise, a function to 'prevent the images
from subjugating (*avassalar*) the field of consciousness'.[36]

Nise also notes that several individuals suffering from
schizophrenia tend to fix their doubles in figures. She uses
Jung's and Freud's notion of 'shadow' to talk about these ob-
scure and rejected parts of the personality. She claims that
the more the elements are repressed, the more the shadow
is nourished and the less it is recognized. For some patients,
such shadows take animal forms; for others, they appear
as monsters or doubles. Generally, the shadow reveals the
conflict within the patient, the self's inner splitting caused
by psychosis.[37] For instance, this is apparent in a specific

---

35 Wilhelm Worringer, *Abstraction and Empathy: A Contribution to the
    Psychology of Style*, trans. by Michael Bullock (Eastford, CT: Martino
    Fine Books, 2014).

36 Silveira, *Imagens do Inconsciente*, p. 28.

37 Following the psychoanalytic framework, the subject (be they neurotic
    or psychotic) is always structured by an inner division (*Spaltung*). In the
    case of psychosis, though, the repressed is rejected towards the outside
    in a very particular way: it takes very concrete and perceptible forms,
    which usually return and are lived as very violent invasions of the inside.

Figure 1. Carlos Pertuis, Untitled, no date, oil on paper.
Image credit: Museu de Imagens do Inconsciente/Museum
of Images from the Unconscious Collection — their archive
is located at the Nise da Silveira Municipal Institute.

work of Abelardo Correia (Figure 2), another patient of the
Section, in which he paints such division: in the reflection
of the mirror held by his right hand, one sees a part of
the self in terror, while the other part, the shadow, holds
a revolver in its left hand. If the shadow opens fire, it will
break the self apart. According to Nise, this image reflects
the very moment of conflict between the two parts of his
self. Indeed, this is a suspended moment: the last thresh-
old has not yet been crossed; his self is not completely
shattered, for the shadow has not taken over. Abelardo's
fragile situation is expressed through his painting. In his
case, the clinical work to be done is to help him resist the
annihilation whose danger inhabits him when he is in this
state.

As with Abelardo, these creative, expressive productions have a double importance as they were regularly exhibited within a museum inside the hospital, thereby con-
structing a substantial archive. They demonstrate Nise's
innovative approach to collective practice and the very
setting it created for the flourishing of artistic works, inas-
much as they let the patients reveal their journeys through
their states, sufferings, and traumas.

AGAINST PHALLOCENTRISM

Nise's relation to psychoanalysis is very complex. She definitely proposes to inscribe herself in this tradition, but not
without proposing amendments to its established framework — in particular regarding the place of the phallus
in psychoanalysis, as well as of the binary coupling of
masculine-feminine. Indeed, I claim that one has to read
her positions by taking into account the very patriarchal
environment in which she develops her work.

Figure 2. Abelardo Correia, Untitled, 1951, graphite and
gouache on paper. Image credit: Museu de Imagens do
Inconsciente/Museum of Images from the Unconscious
Collection — their archive is located at the Nise da Silveira
Municipal Institute.

Throughout Nise's psychiatric practice, Jung is, also for such reasons, an indisputable central reference. Generally, she takes over many of his notions as working tools: the 'collective unconscious' provides the basis for an archaeological drive and social theory of the psyche. Jung's 'archetypes' — for example, the 'great mother' — help her read the patients' productions. Archetypes are used for a comparative anatomy of the psyche, since for Nise, as for Spinoza, the psyche and the body correspond to two forms of expression of one and the same substance, and therefore have logics that are certainly different but comparable. By putting together different individual cases in which similar images appear, it is possible, according to her, to show to the individual that although their suffering belongs to them, they are not alone. This is a struggle that others have already faced, perhaps by going through very archaic journeys, some of which are represented in ancient myths. In this respect, my hypothesis is that her use of mythology can be read as a clinical strategy for the de-dramatization of the pathology and of the hallucinations of the subject.

Last but not least, Nise's return to Jung seems to be strategic to rethink the unconscious in a less phallocentric key:

> And when he [Freud] looks [in *Totem and Taboo*], on this dark continent, for something specific to the little girl, the fundamental element he finds is the envy of the male organ from which the whole psychic development of the woman follows. Everything happens as if the woman were a failed man. [...] With C. G. Jung's psychology, the feminine has its full place and is particularly highlighted. The Jungian unconscious is the mother in a wide symbolic sense, both fascinating and threatening.[38]

---

38   Ibid., p. 276.

Nise mobilizes Jung to make the structural matrix of the unconscious 'the (great) mother'. Such a reversal has clinical
and theoretical implications that demand further analysis
beyond the scope of this paper. Though Jung still refers
to the woman as the feminine and the mother, thereby
maintaining a very problematic binarism, one can see its
inversion in Nise's political operation: a woman — who
chose not to become a mother and dedicated her whole
life to a radical and experimental clinical attempt — situated in post-Vargas Brazil and engaged with struggles for
redefining the very theoretical core and framework of
psychoanalysis. Such an operation against phallocentrism
must thus be read against the very patriarchal environment
in which she worked and the more European established
forms of psychoanalysis.

CONCLUSION

As this essay briefly outlines, Nise's work could make a
significant contribution to the history of radical and critical psychiatry and have global relevance for the future.
More than pointing out whether Nise belongs to this or
that school — Jungian rather than Lacanian or Freudian,
for example —, I argue that she *instrumentalizes* such readings in a very productive manner and transforms them
into working tools for her critical practice and reflection.
Engaging with a variety of European thinkers within and
through her situatedness within Brazil, Nise produces a
deeply innovative and reflective practice. Hence, she unsettles established theoretical frameworks in psychiatry
and psychoanalysis without rejecting them altogether: she
reconfigures unorthodox concepts coming from polemical streams of psychoanalysis; she thinks very early about
how to use unconventional elements in the clinical setting

(such as animals, for example); she transforms artistic expression into the core of the treatment of mental disorder and discards more medicalized strategies.

Nise's work has slowly started to gain some visibility but, given the innovativeness of her critical interventions in psychiatry, this remains very far from what her legacy merits. Two recent examples confirm this point. First, there is the 11th Berlin Biennale, held in the fall of 2020, which had a room dedicated to her and some of her patients' works. Unfortunately, it was poorly exhibited in a narrow room, cornered among unrelated rooms, and without enough contextualization. Second, a more comprehensive exhibition, titled *Images from the Unconscious*, took place at Marres in Maastricht in the spring of 2022. It presented a very prominent corpus of works by three famous artists of the Section: Adelina Gomes (Figure 3), Carlos Pertuis, and Fernando Diniz. However, due to a lack of interest from other European institutions, the exhibition did not travel, and the works went straight back to Brazil. Indeed, one could also add that, despite all her connections to important European figures such as Ronald Laing, Henri Ey, or Jung since the 1950s, her writings have remained mostly untranslated into other languages. This is the case not only with Nise's works but also with other significant Brazilian figures such as Osório César and Mário Pedrosa.

Years before Anti-Psychiatry, which flourished in the 1960 and 1970s, a psychiatrist within an authoritarian Global South context was already practicing radical and critical alternative strategies of care. Today, in the highly medicalized times we live in, marked by a renewed organicist vision of mental disorders, coming back to Nise's reflections and practices — as well as to the Brazilian history of psychiatry and psychoanalysis — would definitely bring fresh and powerful perspectives to current clinical debates.

Figure 3. Adelina Gomes, *Untitled* ('Great Mother' series),
1940s, modelling clay for plaster cast. Image credit: Museu
de Imagens do Inconsciente/Museum of Images from the
Unconscious Collection — their archive is located at the
Nise da Silveira Municipal Institute.

Kill your Darlings (Working Title)
KATA KATZ

Inspired by Virginia Woolf's writing technique of following a stream of consciousness, I aim to create a text that reflects on the very process of exploring an idea, bearing witness to how ideas grow and eventually leap into actuality. Thus, I step into a stream of thoughts and try to find a beginning, (re-)visiting ideas from the past and the present that occupy my mind rent-free.

'Kill your Darlings' — a phrase which I have to admit I never gave much consideration. It appears as a clear message, or I thought it would. For me, it meant that we should be able to leave our idols, professional or otherwise, behind us. Learn to let go of and detach ourselves from the umbilical cord, so to speak. Thus, it is a perfect fit for my title, even if it is a bit too catchy for the current think piece. The phrase has an Oedipal ring to it, and my interpretation of it as killing off the father figure made me look into it deeper only to find out that, indeed, my assumption was incorrect, although not too far from the original meaning.

'Kill your darlings' is often a piece of advice one receives from experienced writers in a manner of a masterclass.

> You kill your darlings when you decide to get rid
> of an unnecessary storyline, character, or sentence
> in a piece of creative writing — elements you may
> have worked hard to create but must be removed
> for the sake of your overall story.[1]

Why is my failing to catch the meaning of this phrase so important? Because for the longest time, I have been curious about how we can produce knowledge differently in order to bend the frames of disciplined processes of thought and hopefully open it to others.

What does it mean to kill your darlings when you see them as your idols? In our contemporary networked culture, an idol refers to a person who is a greatly admired role model since they cannot fail by any means. Our patriarchal academic practice loves producing these idols whose works shine some celestial light upon us and treating them like geniuses. Indeed, a person who is constructed in terms of such intellectual power is assumed to be born with this gift. Their gift is seen as 'natural' or god-given, as if they were blessed with it. Not surprisingly, men most often have taken this name and position, whereas the woman, the Other, the sinner, falling from grace, is rarely seen as a genius. But why is this role assigned to women, and to everyone whose existence challenges the (gender) binary system? Taking it a step further: why do we even need geniuses in the first place?

Despite the ever-continuing, if not expanding, war raging on science and women via a conservative politics on the rise (again), feminist, queer, and decolonial theories try to hold their ground strong while coming from the margins. Since current academia and its epistemic regimes

---

1   'What Does It Mean to Kill Your Darlings?', *MasterClass*, 8 September 2021 <https://www.masterclass.com/articles/what-does-it-mean-to-kill-your-darlings> [accessed 21 December 2022].

are still products of the overbearing patriarchal culture, I would like to tackle the myth(s) of knowledge production that this culture reproduces. I grew up in Catholic Hungary, surrounded by Christian mythology. In this respect, my first gesture would be to connect the tropes of the intellectual role model with two myths: that of the genius and that of the banning of Adam and Eve from Eden. More specifically, I am interested in what kind of connection one can find between the myth of an exile from Eden and the male genius. In this respect, the striking aspect of the myth is that it condemns one more than the other. For instance, due to childbirth and menstruation, women are sentenced to greater physical pain and on top of that to be governed by men. Thus, a woman who curiously seeks knowledge becomes the Other-ed, categorized as a transgressor to be tamed and repressed. The underlying message here is to be wary of curiosity and change as much as it is to distrust what one recognizes as the Other — the woman. Only knowledge derived from a deified figure can be valid and trustworthy. The authority of this figure of superiority, the man, cannot be questioned — like the establishment itself. Through these cultural threads, even implicitly, the model of the genius has not surprisingly become associated with the male, mainly white figure.

Then, who is the idol that I am fighting here? Am I contesting the mechanisms that constitute these god-like idols? Should I dig into these idols as symptoms of the contemporary knowledge cultures and power asymmetries that are within them? But really, what kind of knowledge is produced by a genius? A singular, self-contained, mythical figure of knowledge-making, as if he were devoid of history, roots, or influences? How does this bubble of omniscience maintain itself as well as the authority of geniuses it hosts? Yet, all these questions indicate a self-justifying image of the genius that does not reflect material and social conditions of knowledge production in the sense of intellectual labour and creativity. This self-justifying image hides away from the cultivation of the community and denies individuals perceived as the Other the right to participate. The authority becomes mystic as much as solid, where canons arise to separate and dominate.

From this perspective, I now interpret the phrase 'kill your darlings' as a call to kill the intellectual geniuses I have been educated with and eventually constrained by. Nothing too bloody or naive, but it is time to question their place and relevance and to let go of their patronage in order to think with others, thereby overcoming universalistic and exclusionary approaches that do not align with the world around me.[2] In a masterclass, allegedly coming from the German *Meisterklasse*, you get the qualification to be a master of your art by being mentored not only by the best intellectuals but by those valued for their way of thinking beyond the disciplinary boundaries and their asymmetrical valuation of knowledge-making traditions. Indeed, the system of the masterclass recognizes that the educational framework can be and should be expanded through the view of 'experts' who offer alternative modes of transmitting one's know-how. Although I do not yet know, and may never know, how to fully escape the narrative of idolatry, seeking mentors who engage in a similar quest, and prioritizing the task of thinking with others, seems like a good place to start.

By drawing on Donna Haraway's and Ursula Le Guin's reflections, I try to be grounded in theories that attempt

---

2   Becoming a feminist killjoy is definitely one way to go to transform the rage and other negative energies. For inspiration and guidance see Sara Ahmed, *The Feminist Killjoy Handbook* (London: Allen Lane, 2023).

to stay open to dialogue, self-reflexivity, and transformation without being overdetermined by exclusivity or judg-
ment.[3] Accordingly, for this current piece I gathered female identifying authors in order to challenge the male-
authors-dominated curriculum I have often encountered in
higher education in Germany and Hungary. For instance,
students are constantly exposed to the works of male
authors and thinkers, and these students come to assume
that the task of intellectual creation is reserved mainly for
men. After I had struggled with gender pronouns in a first
language that doesn't use them, the educational setting
in German and English, languages with gender pronouns,
more clearly exposed how students most of the time assume that the author is He, a male. The globally growing
trend of diversifying the curriculum (e.g. decolonizing the
curriculum) has also reached here in Berlin, but in what
capacity? What are the potentials and challenges that await
us? The framing of 'us' here refers to the cultural and academic workers teaching and researching in Germany, a
country that has hardly come to terms with its colonial
history and present.

Thus, I propose to focus on authors who can guide me
while I address all these questions, which are layered and
complicated enough. I organize them in a list format to
highlight their processual methods of thinking that allow
incompleteness and growth, since learning with others is
a never-ending endeavour (for me). In other words, this is
my first attempt at a draft for a masterclass I would like to
attend.

3   See Ursula K. Le Guin, 'The Carrier Bag Theory of Fiction', in *Carrier
     Bag Fiction*, ed. by Sarah Shin and Matthias Zeiske (Leipzig: Spector
     Books, 2021), pp. 34–44, and Donna J. Haraway, *Manifestly Haraway*
     (Minneapolis: University of Minnesota Press, 2016).

Speaking nearby: Trinh Minh-ha beautifully describes how she tries to escape the so-called objective world built by the white man. She reflects on the historical construction of man as the all-knowing subject of knowledge and truth that is allowed to speak for/on behalf of everyone else. Her strategy is simple yet effective: She alienates the white man as she freely plays with his thoughts, which she displays without naming them. She points out that man's obsession with objectivity is actually a delusion produced by a positivist dream of neutrality. Trinh gestures at 'a continuation striving for continuation' rather than totalization — her voice is not the only one but speaks among many; she does not speak about but nearby.[4] Following her reasoning, there is no writing that would not refer to other texts; there is no I nor you to come first. Then, the act of writing creates a dialogical encounter through which one can recognize the relationality of self as a prism of reflection that necessarily implies collectivity as much as connectivity.[5]

Speculative thinking: Sadie Plant gathers different facts and quotes to create 'connectedness across time and space' as if 'weaving different textures together'.[6] Through her protagonists, she weaves threads of speculation by interlinking history, science, and fiction. When I first read her book, I held it in my hand as an academic text that was serious and professional. Shortly afterward, I visited an exhibition inspired by the book and changed my perception of it to a fictional novel. Even though this revelation irritated me, I soon realized that this gesture of combin-

---

4   Trinh T. Minh-ha, *Woman, Native, Other: Writing Postcoloniality and Feminism* (Bloomington: Indiana University Press, 1989), p. 49.

5   Ibid.

6   Sadie Plant, *Zeros and Ones: Digital Women and the New Technoculture* (London: Fourth Estate, 1995), p. 15.

ing fiction and academic standards fascinated me all along. Isn't it the sheer display of free thinking that appealed to my intellect? When I read her book, I dreamed of forming a friendship with Plant's protagonists, Ada and Eve.[7]

Critical fabulation: Saidiya Hartman's concept of critical fabulation is an exemplary approach for scholars who seek to appropriate fiction to create a historical reality for those whose existence has been denied for too long. By re-enacting the phantom experience of the overlooked and unseen, Hartman not only explores what they might have been but also deconstructs and reformulates the tropes of (official) history-writing. The act of fabulation, registering the absent presence of those left out of official histories, disrupts the conventions of the archive and of history-writing that have been built upon the white man's claims to truth under the guise of objectivity. Indeed, her critical, fact-based fabulation reveals that the voice of the oppressed was always dominated by the oppressor even when included within the text. In other words, the oppressor dominated the narration of reality by means of silencing and speaking on behalf of the other. The author, a descendant of the oppressed, reformulates as much as she deconstructs the tools of the oppressor to find her voice beyond this colonial, binary logic that reduces her to the role of the oppressed. Hence, Hartman's theoretical work gains political relevance by blurring the boundaries between categories, such as reality and fiction, and thus dismantling the system of opposites.[8]

Cosmopolitan science: Anna Tsing argues that we have to reopen our imagination to a 'cosmopolitan sci-

7   Ibid.
8   Saidiya Hartman, *Venus in Two Acts* (New York: Cassandra Press, 2021).

ence' that is composed of patches rather than constituted by totalizing domination. In this approach, academic discourse and its epistemic regimes embrace their relational, incomplete nature as part of a large, shifting multitude. While researching the globalized commodity chains of matsutake mushrooms across national borders and scientific paradigms, Tsing engages with multiple and sometimes conflicting practices and motivations of different stakeholders, farmers, amateurs, contributors, and sellers. For her, scientists should stay open to an encounter with the varied aspects of so-called shared reality and the heterogeneity through which even totalizing systems like capitalism operate. Not surprisingly, Tsing situates her work at the expanding edges of academic discourse by experimenting with writing styles, too. For example, she incorporates proses that bring forth her voice as well as the poetic nature of living and knowing. What fascinates me is the very gesture of sharing knowledge in an accessible, demystifying language as she evokes fictions and narratives historically tied to a community, a collective.[9]

Radical scholarly praxis: Katherine McKittrick reflects not on the genius-being of one person but on the collective that has nourished that creativity. For instance, I like her listing of the names that have influenced her work right at the beginning of the book. When she describes what she calls 'radical scholarly praxis' as inquiring about something 'unknown, unnamed, unbound', McKittrick underscores the possibilities of thinking outside the established Euro-American white supremacist culture that is internalized and normalized to the point that it hides its

---

9   Anna L. Tsing, *The Mushroom at the End of the World: On the Possibilities of Life in Capitalist Ruins* (Princeton, NJ: Princeton University Press, 2015).

own historical constructedness. An ignorance that stems from privilege fails to see that there is nothing more fictitious than our understanding of reality itself. Seeking poetry in thinking/theorizing motivates us to embrace the fictive and incomplete nature of objectivity as much as subjectivity. The question I ask is: Can a scientific practice that cannot accept any realities other than those it describes call itself a scientific practice?[10]

In this text, I reflect on how my thoughts develop in the entangled process of writing and thinking, and I ask myself again and again: Why is my tone so angry? Am I going to keep this tone forever, or will writing help me heal, too? It is hard to escape the long-lasting legacies that surround us and shape our understanding of what constitutes theorization, especially when the already-should-be-here structural changes are still too far away despite all the victories.

The list above demonstrates various ways of killing the god-like idols of academia or theory at large. These ways involve speaking, listening, and thinking nearby. They are open to being challenged. Indeed, they challenge themselves in every corner of their research and books because they know well that not being challenged means missing out on the epistemological benefits of failure and the freedom of not knowing 'completely'.

This manner of thinking is expressed not only as freedom but as a beauty that flourishes in one's openness to new encounters and the reality of the unknown, the unknowability of the world, others, and ourselves, never isolated and stable. So, how do I deal with epistemic legacies that have constituted me without totally abandoning them? How to not only reconfigure the asymmetries

---

10   Katherine McKittrick, *Dear Science and Other Stories* (Durham, NC: Duke University Press, 2021).

they keep reproducing but also generate new modes of community-building?

Eventually, my rage was channelled into a project that advocates cultivating what I call, alongside my colleague Mafalda Sandrini, cultures of failure within academia. For instance, this agenda may involve acknowledging the possible epistemological benefits of scientific errors or critically reflecting on the structural precarity embedded within the academic career that fails to provide fair means of working and living for scholars. This project has taught me to allow myself to heal with others while laughing, crying, and thinking with them. We fail nearby each other and seek small hacks to counter the mechanisms of academia that often economically and sometimes intellectually marginalize us, early career scholars, and find ways to implement the seeds of change.

My conclusion so far is that we need to learn to let go of ideas that serve only a few and adopt a practice of canonization that allows for these canons to be reshaped by practicing, first and foremost, what I call attempted murder on the loop: killing darlings. For let us not be naive, these geniuses will not disappear so easily. We need to create alternative systems of canons as Le Guin describes so beautifully in 'The Carrier Bag Theory of Fiction'. These are not just stories but stories with the figure of a hero, which is to say, we need to dismantle the normative formations, such as patriarchy, that maintain this image of the self-contained figure of authority that monopolizes claims to truth. Indeed, it is not enough to kill our idols since idols are not the problem per se; they could only be symptoms. So, why not just put them in the carrier bag of theories? We cannot forget them, but we can multiply stories to the extent that they lose their dominance so that we can open up new trajectories for relating and knowing. For sure, it will first be necessary to form something like a counter-canon, which mimics killing. But ultimately the point is not to 'kill' but to 'multiply'.

I first learned about the concept of the carrier bag from Le Guin's *The Word for World is Forest*.[11] I learned it through the actions of her protagonists, not by her naming what she was doing; then I forgot it and learned it again. She imagined the way of knowledge in the World of Athshe, where learning and knowing is based on the needs of the collective. Before the colonizers came, Athsheans lived in a peaceful society, in harmony with their surroundings, not knowing what killing or violence meant. They share a collective memory entangled by everything living. Hence, they cannot forget the killing that man has brought with him, but they can choose not to act on it; their organizing principle of life is based on the needs of the collective and they choose to leave violence untouched in their bag of knowledge, as they decided they have no need for it.

Ultimately, we need to undertake the task of reconfiguring how we value alternative modes of knowledge and creativity within academia. For instance, we can re-evaluate the place of fiction in our research practices, move towards a cosmopolitan science composed of patches — as Anna Tsing describes it — and question the assumed homogeneity of the logic underlying exclusive claims to universality. We can advocate institutional infrastructures for egalitarian, collaborative settings of knowledge production. We can reject the mystifications through which the kingdoms of experts and geniuses endure. Keep failing! In doing so, embrace failure's many facets and use them. Keep questioning, forgetting, learning, and relearning, not neces-

---

11   Ursula K. Le Guin, *The Word for World Is Forest* (New York: TOR, 1972).

sarily in that order, but always with others. In this sense, I want to close this text by saying that it has been a pleasure to think with you, Eylül, Ira, Jakka, Juliana, Mahmoud, Fred, Şirin, Michela, Bruna, Ana Carolina, Nader, Firoozeh, Bernardo, Marlon. Being part of this collective extended the stories, widening my bag of theories and making room for all those narratives that are otherwise pushed to the margins. And my hopes are, I could do the same for you.

Making Germany's Hidden Yet Omnipresent Colonial Past Visible

ANA CAROLINA SCHVEITZER

Since I moved to the German capital in 2018, I have heard the following statement on a regular basis: Berlin is a multicultural city. There is even a German slang term to refer to Berlin: *Multikulti*. With the recent wave of migration, Berlin has become known for embracing its diverse communities. Yet, this impression is only partially valid. Historically, many groups have been marginalized and their histories silenced. Even today, most of Berlin's museums present a selected view of the country's history, mainly focusing on white German protagonists. In the case of museums with non-European collections, such as the famous Pergamon Museum or the Neues Museum, visitors learn very little about how these objects ended up in this city. Walking through Berlin nowadays, one can learn about the history of the Berlin Wall, the process of reunification, the World Wars, and the tragedy of the Holocaust. However, there is a lack of knowledge regarding the city's ties to German colonialism.

This text is a walking tour through the city of Berlin. I would like to invite you to look at different parts of the city to unpack the residues of Germany's colonial past, an overlooked theme in German official history.

Let's start.

FIRST STOP — WILHELMSTRAßE 92

If you have ever been to Berlin, you have likely visited this spot. It is just a seven-minute walk from the Brandenburg Gate. On 15 November 1884, it was here that the Congo Conference started in a government building that no longer exists. Otto von Bismarck, the first German chancellor, invited leaders from thirteen nations in Europe and the United States to discuss the colonial policy related to African territories. The conference dispersed, after four months, at the end of February 1885.

The agreements made by imperial powers, including Germany, allowed them to expand their presence in the African continent and further undermine African sovereignty: European nations occupied and divided African territories while establishing new borders that aligned with their colonial projections.[1] Colonial administrations and private companies established a system to extract resources available in the continent while relying on forced labour and extreme conditions of exploitation. The long-term effects of such European colonialist expansion have been felt in the economic, political, and cultural sectors throughout the twentieth century and persist until today.

Indeed, Germany had an active role in this process, for the agreements established during this event — later

---

[1]   *Archives of Empire*, ed. by Barbara Harlow and Mia Carter, 2 vols (Durham, NC: Duke University Press, 2003–04), ii: *The Scramble for Africa* (2004).

called the Berlin Conference — helped to build its overseas empire. From 1884 to 1914, Germany had four colonies in Africa and some protectorates in Asia.[2] Among its
motivations, Germany had a strong interest in expanding
its territories and competing with other imperial powers;
moreover, it had the support of companies to further develop its colonial project. The usual narratives of German
colonialism focus on the economic aspects of the former
colonies. In this kind of economic narrative, the colony of
German Togo, which nowadays corresponds to the countries of Togo and (a small part of) Ghana, is portrayed as a
region solely dedicated to the exportation of palm oil and
palm kerns.[3] Or, German Cameroon, which today corresponds to the countries of the Republic of Cameroon, (part
of) Gabon, and the Republic of the Congo, is reduced to
a site of cocoa cultivation and the exploration of rubber.
However, the colonial agenda reached far beyond the mere
exploitation of natural resources. Studies have shown that
this was only possible through extensive violence and the
forced exploitation of African labour force.[4]

---

2   In the Pacific, Germany controlled German New Guinea, part of Samoa,
     the Bismarck Archipelago, the German Solomon Islands Protector-
     ate, and Kiautschou Bay (located in China). For a brief overview of
     German colonialism, see Sebastian Conrad, 'Rethinking German Co-
     lonialism in a Global Age', *The Journal of Imperial and Commonwealth
     History*, 41 (2013), pp. 543–66 <https://doi.org/10.1080/03086534.
     2013.836352>.

3   Peter Sebald, *Die deutsche Kolonie Togo 1884–1914: Auswirkungen einer
     Fremdherrschaft* (Berlin: C. Links, 2013).

4   To give an example, Oestermann's book deeply analyses the exploit-
     ation of African workers in the rubber industry in German Cameroon.
     It demonstrates how the extraction of this colonial commodity by
     companies was only possible due to an extensive use of the African la-
     bour force. See Tristan Oestermann, *Kautschuk und Arbeit in Kamerun
     unter deutscher Kolonialherrschaft 1880–1913* (Vienna: Böhlau Verlag,
     2023).

Hence, German colonies also became sites of conflict and resistance. More specifically, two colonies experienced brutal wars under the German administration. In the former German East Africa, which comprised the present-day states of Tanzania, Burundi, and Rwanda, at least 100,000 Africans died between 1905 and 1908 in the Maji-Maji war.[5] They were first killed by German military violence during the conflict, and then by a devastating famine following the war. The conflict started in the south of Tanzania as a reaction to almost one decade of labour force exploitation/forced labour and abusive head taxes implemented by the German colonial authorities.[6]

Another brutal war took place in German South-West Africa, which today corresponds to the territory of Namibia. This colony became the only settler colony of the German Empire as many Germans moved to these occupied lands. What happened from 1904 to 1908 in this colony is very hard to describe. German authorities led by Gen. Lothar von Trotha — and I believe we must name the responsible — decided not to have war prisoners. Therefore, as a result of his decision, all those who fought against Germans would have to be killed. Herero and Nama — men, women, and children — were thus forced to march through the Omaheke Desert. Later, Germans created concentration camps, where all the survivors were forced to work. Around 80% of the Herero were massacred, and this is now considered the first genocide of the twentieth century. What happened to the Herero and Nama in Namibia

---

5   James Giblin and Jamie Monson, *Maji Maji: Lifting the Fog of War* (Leiden: Brill, 2010).

6   Thaddeus Sunseri, 'The Maji-Maji War, 1905–1907', in *Oxford Research Encyclopedia of African History*, ed. by Thomas Spear (Oxford: Oxford University Press, 2022), pp. 1–40 <https://doi.org/10.1093/acrefore/9780190277734.013.154>.

under German rule remains shocking. Only in 2021, more than one hundred years later, did Germany officially recognize this event as a genocide. There was more than one century of silence.

Anticolonial resistance was present since the early years of colonialism. Kinjikitile Ngwale, a member of the Matumbi people and one of the first leaders of the Maji-Maji war, was killed in the first year of the conflict. Samuel Maharero and Hendrik Witbooi, Herero and Nama chiefs, became a symbol of anti-colonial struggles in Namibia. Even the Namibian dollar has Witbooi's portrait on the surface. Yet, these names are absent from German official history, such as school textbooks.

As summarized above, the Berlin Conference changed the course of colonialism and the futures of African states, but what we find today at Wilhelmstraße 92 is an inversely proportional representation. For years, the only thing you could find here was a plaque referring to it as a historical marker. The plaque carries a text available in German, English, and French — colonial languages only— in which a short paragraph reminds us of the importance of remembering the violence of a colonial past. Besides this text, one can see three images: a photograph of the former building façade, an 1883 drawing of the conference, and a photo of people in chains, the victims of the genocide promoted by the Germans in Namibia between 1904 and 1908.

Unfortunately, there is little information on the scene about the effects of this conference. The photos of the victims denounce the fact that thirty years of German colonialism left no positive legacy. But since the plaque has not been given much visibility, it is likely that thousands of people have passed by it without ever noticing it.

However, things have changed since I arrived in Berlin in 2018. Most recently, in 2020, different initiatives came together and created a pilot project called 'Dekoloniale Memory Culture in the City'. Located exactly at Wilhelm-straße 92, it represents a 'recovery of this historical place'.[7] The three initiatives that coordinate this project are *Berlin Postkolonial e. V.*, Each One Teach One (EOTO) *e. V.*, and *Initiative Schwarze Menschen in Deutschland* (*ISD-Bund e. V.*).[8] The project aims to highlight Berlin's responsibilities as a former colonial metropole and imperial capital. To do so, the organizations have put together scholars, activists, and artists to create new spaces or intervene in historical ones. Moreover, they renarrate the urban history of Berlin as a city where significant migrant diasporic communities from different (post)colonial contexts have resided.

In 2022, the 12th Berlin Biennale focused on address-ing the question of how 'colonialism and imperialism con-tinue to operate in the present', and used the space as one of its venues.[9] During the biennale, the street windows of the location became part of a public installation by Nil Yalter, a Turkish contemporary feminist artist living in Europe, titled *EXILE IS A HARD JOB* (1983/2022) (Fig-ure 1). The same statement, which gave the work its title, was painted on the windows in languages, such as Turkish and Arabic, that are predominantly used by the immigrant population in the city.

As these collaborations demonstrate, Dekoloniale's main goal is to disclose the hidden yet omnipresent Ger-man colonial past, promoting conversations and actions

---

7   'About Us', Dekoloniale Memory Culture in the City website: <https://www.dekoloniale.de/en/about> [accessed 2 January 2023]

8   In German, 'e. V.' refers to 'eingetragener Verein', which can be trans-lated into English as 'registered association'.

9   'About the 12th Berlin Biennale for Contemporary Art', Berlin Biennale for Contemporary Art website, 2022 <https://12.berlinbiennale.de/about/> [accessed 23 January 2023].

Figure 1. Nil Yalter, EXILE IS A HARD JOB, 1983/2022, postering workshop with Nagham Hammoush and Rüzgâr Buşki. Installation view: 'Dekoloniale Memory Culture in the City', 12th Berlin Biennale for Contemporary Art, 11 June–18 September 2022. Image credit: photo by Silke Briel.

about it in the present. Indeed, these collaborations understand colonialism as a system of injustices against which many people from the colonized regions have been fighting, and it is this ongoing struggle that resonates with those fighting against racism in contemporary German society. As Berlin is a former colonial metropole and a present hub of migrants, the cultural institutions within the city have the responsibility of unpacking its colonial past. To this end, the initiatives involved with Dekoloniale try to address three central themes — memory, visibility, and diversity — by organizing public programmes to reach out to a larger audience. Our first stop, Wilhelmstraße 92, is included in the cinematic and digital city walk that Dekoloniale has organized. 'Agitprop' is the name of a current initiative in which Dekoloniale offers a residency programme for artists, designers, and writers. This year, it will concentrate on the districts of Charlottenburg and Wilmersdorf. The outcome is a collaborative exhibition to be held in 2023.

The efforts of this project touch different parts of the city, so let's follow our itinerary and visit some of these spaces.

SECOND STOP — TREPTOWER PARK AND
TREPTOW-KÖPENICK

We are now going out of the ring area to visit our second spot: Treptower Park. People usually visit it to see the Soviet War Memorial, built in 1949, which is not our focus now. Here, more than one hundred years ago, a human zoo was set. However, today the park bears not a single trace of this event. The colonial memory has once again been removed from the view.

In the summer of 1896, almost 7.5 million people went to the city's Treptower Park to visit the First German Colonial Exhibition.[10] Visitors paid sixty cents to entertain themselves at the expense of almost 106 people (women, men, and children) from the former German colonies who were exploitatively exhibited there. These people were put on display, with a space demarcating where they had to

---

10   Robbie Aitken, 'The First German Colonial Exhibition (1896)', Black Central Europe Studies Network (BCESN) <https:// blackcentraleurope.com/sources/1850-1914/the-first-german-colonial-exhibition-1896/> [accessed 2 January 2023].

stand, as if in a zoo. For almost six months, every day, they were featured as part of the event's attractions. Besides the humiliating conditions to which they were exposed, they were offered no appropriate accommodation during their stay in the German capital.

At that time, they used the word *Völkerschau* to describe this event, which could be translated into English as 'ethnic show'. By exposing people and making money in the process, Germany not only objectified the victims but also commodified them. As a large-scale event, the First German Colonial Exhibition was built with the cooperation of many actors and involved politicians, businessmen, clergy, and staff from ethnological and natural science museums. Thus, this historical incidence demonstrates how these institutions reinforce the idea that the colonized people are the 'exotics', the ones to be observed, classified, and studied. As defined by Sandra Koutsoukos, these expositions became 'humiliating spectacles of difference',[11] reaffirming racist ideas according to which the people of these regions were both inferior and exotic.

In order to bring back this part of the city's history and to highlight the many people affected by the exhibitions, since 2017 the Museum Treptow-Köpenick has been hosting the exhibition 'Looking Back — *zurückgeschaut*'.[12] The exhibition is dedicated to telling the stories of these 106 people who worked in the First German Colonial Exhibition. In addition to naming these people and tracing some of their life trajectories during and in the aftermath of the 1896 exhibition, visitors can also get a broader picture of thirty

---

11   Sandra Sofia Machado Koutsoukos, *Zoológicos humanos: gente em exibição na era do imperialismo* (Campinas: Editora da Universidade Estadual de Campinas, 2020), p. 24.

12   Museum Treptow, Exhibition: '*zurückgeschaut | Looking back*: Die Erste Deutsche Kolonialausstellung von 1896 in Berlin-Treptow' <https://www.berlin.de/museum-treptow-koepenick/ausstellungen/artikel.649851.php> [accessed 3 January 2023].

years of German colonialism. The project is the outcome of a cooperation between initiatives such as *Berlin Postkolonial (e. V.)* and *Initiative Schwarze Menschen* (Initiative of Black People in Germany). After a few months of being closed for renovations, the exhibition reopened in October 2021 and became the first permanent exhibition on colonialism, racism, and black resistance in a Berlin museum.

THIRD STOP — AFRICAN QUARTER IN WEDDING

Even though in Treptower Park the vestiges of German colonialism are erased, many survive in the neighbourhood of Wedding. Between 1900 and 1958, the streets and squares around Seestraße and Müllerstraße were renamed. The names chosen refer to former German colonies and individuals who played an important role in German colonial politics. For instance, it is in this part of Berlin that Togostraße (Togo Street) intersects with Sansibarstraße (Zanzibar Street), and Swakopmunder (the name of a town in Namibia) meets Ghanastraße (Ghana Street).

However, it is also here that we find Petersallee (Peters Avenue), named after Carl Peters. As a businessman, he was deeply involved in German colonial politics and held an important position in the German East Africa Company. Petersallee represents the elite that got rich from colonial exploitation. Very similar is the story of Lüderitzstraße, which relates to Adolf Lüderitz, a German merchant who bought an island to the south of Namibia in 1883, marking the beginning of the German occupation in the region. These streets received these names before the First World War, when Germany still had colonies abroad. Today, they symbolize vestiges of the colonial past.

It is not new that many groups have been fighting to change the names of streets, squares, and underground stations in Berlin. Tanzanian-born Mnyaka Sururu Mboro, who has lived in Berlin for more than three decades, is one of the most active in these movements.[13] Besides his commitment to reparation and restitution efforts regarding past colonies of Germany, such as Tanzania, Mboro promotes walking tours through the neighbourhood, connecting the colonial past and explaining the names of the streets.

While I am writing this piece, the African Quarter appears again as a topic in the German newspapers.[14] Nachtigalplatz, originally named to celebrate the colonialist Gustav Nachtigal, has been renamed Manga-Bell-Platz to remember the Duala royal couple, Emily and Rudolf Manga Bell, who fought against German colonial rule in Cameroon.[15] In addition, Lüderitzstraße became Cornelius-Fredericks-Straße, the name of an important leader who fought against the German forces during the Herero and Namaqua War (1904–07). It is important to highlight that these decisions for renaming these places took place thanks to efforts by the initiatives briefly described here. Other suggestions include the names of South African singer Miriam Makeba; Queen Nzinga, who controlled the ancient kingdoms of Ndongo and Matamba

13   Johannes Odenthal and Judith Weber, Profile of Mnyaka Sururu Mboro, Koloniales Erbe Project Website, 2018 <https://www.adk.de/de/projekte/2018/koloniales-erbe/symposium-I/teilnehmer/mnyaka-sururu-mboro.htm> [accessed 27 December 2022].

14   Birgit Lotze, 'Afrikanisches Viertel: Deshalb werden Straßen umbenannt', Berliner Morgenpost, 29 November 2022 <https://www.morgenpost.de/bezirke/mitte/article237030899/Wechsel-im-Afrikanischen-Viertel.html> [accessed 14 December 2022].

15   The Museum am Rothenbaum — Kulturen und Künste der Welt (MARKK), in Hamburg, has an excellent exhibition on the life of Rudolf Manga Bell. See: Museum am Rothenbaum — Kulturen und Künste der Welt, 'Hey Hamburg, do you know Duala Manga Bell?', exhibition website: <https://markk-hamburg.de/ausstellungen/hey-hamburg/> [accessed 14 December 2022].

(today Angola); and the first African Nobel Peace Prize winner, Wangari Maathai.[16] It is striking that many residents and businesses in these neighbourhoods complain about their address details being changed. These complaints do not diminish the symbolic importance of such changes. Indeed, they underline the urgent need to take more concrete steps towards city-wide decolonization efforts on both official and public terms.

It is time to go to the last stop.

LAST STOP — HUMBOLDT FORUM

So, now we go back to the main street: Unter den Linden. We are standing in front of a new old palace. Yes, you have read it right: 'new old'. The Humboldt Forum is located at the Berliner Palace, which was the royal residence from 1443 to 1918. The bombings of the two World Wars left the structure in disrepair and the administration of the German Democratic Republic decided to demolish it. Later, they erected the Palace of the Republic and called it the 'People's Palace'. From 1976 to 1990, the building hosted significant cultural, political, social, and academic events and became a symbol of East Germany in the heart of Berlin.

In October 1990, the Palace of the Republic was closed to visitors due to its contamination with asbestos. Twelve years after the reunification, in 2002, the German parliament voted not only to demolish the building but also to construct a new cultural complex. This was a very controversial decision since it meant destroying an East German

---

16   To see the complete list: 'Informationen rund um die Straßenumbenennungen im Afrikanischen Viertel im Wedding, Berlin-Mitte', Bezirksamt Mitte: Fachbereich Kunst, Kultur und Geschichte <https://www.berlin.de/kunst-und-kultur-mitte/geschichte/afrikanisches-viertel-609903.php> [accessed 10 January 2023].

monument, erasing a thick layer of city memory. After spending twenty years and almost €680 million, the new building opened its doors to the public.

Now, we are here looking at a majestic palace. There is even a cross placed on the top of its dome. For some, this created controversy for glorifying the German colonial legacy and undermining the religious diversity of the communities that make up Berlin today. Now you might ask me, how does this connect with Germany's colonial past? Why is this the last stop on our tour? The answer is the collection it harbours. The Humboldt Forum is the newest museum on Museum Island and holds the collections of the former Ethnological Museum of Berlin and the Museum of Asian Art.

In recent years, there has been widespread criticism of this new museum.[17] The book *No Humboldt 21!* is an

---

17 The construction of the Berlin City Palace and the creation of the Humboldt Forum have been the topic of many debates. Regarding the construction, the history of the palace, and the erasing of vestiges of the German Democratic Republic (GDR), see Carol Anne Costabile-Heming, 'The Reconstructed City Palace and Humboldt Forum in Berlin: Restoring Architectural Identity or Distorting the Memory of Historic Spaces?', *Journal of Contemporary European Studies*, 25 (2017), pp. 441–54. Scholars have focused on the case of the Humboldt Forum to raise questions about the role of museums and ethnological collections. See Margareta von Oswald, *Working Through Colonial Collections: 'Africa' in Berlin's Humboldt Forum* (Leuven: Leuven University Press, 2022). On the debates on the restitution of African artefacts, provenance research, and the controversy around the colonial legacy of the Humboldt Forum, see Fatima El-Tayeb, 'The Universal Museum: How the New Germany Built its Future on Colonial Amnesia', *Nka: Journal of Contemporary African Art*, 46 (2020), pp. 72–82; Daniel Morat, 'Katalysator wider Willen: Das Humboldt Forum in Berlin und die deutsche Kolonialvergangenheit', *Zeithistorische Forschungen — Studies in Contemporary History*, 16 (2019), pp. 140–53; and George Okello Abungu, 'Die Frage nach Restitution und Rückgabe: Ein Dialog der Interessen', in *(Post)Kolonialismus und Kulturelles Erbe: Internationale Debatten im Humboldt Forum*, ed. by Dortje Fink and Martina Urioste-Buschmann (Munich: Hanser, 2021), pp. 110–31.

outcome of these critiques.[18] Published in 2018, the manuscript brings together interviews, essays, and images resulting from the campaign with the same name, co-sponsored by AfricAvenir. This essay collection problematizes the reconstruction of the palace as a survival and celebration of imperialist culture. Authors (scholars and activists) also make demands for restitution and point out the urgency of an equal dialogue that considers the colonial heritage of this new museum. With the slogan 'Tear it down and turn it upside down', The Coalition of Cultural Workers against the Humboldt Forum (CCWAH) mobilized around these critiques and these demands for restitution in the case of Humboldt Forum. The participation of cultural workers is crucial because they address how the Humboldt Forum owns many items stolen during Germany's colonial era. Moreover, they call their colleagues to take responsibility, as cultural workers, for decolonizing cultural institutions. A fascinating example is the campaign 'I won't participate because…', where they pointed out why collaborating with the Humboldt Forum is far from being a good idea.

Indeed, the opening of the Humboldt Forum has been received by many as a significant obstacle to the process of repatriation of African objects. These protests and debates created public awareness around these issues, which the institution addressed by restructuring the display of the items that were relocated from the ethnographic museum collections. For example, informative texts about colonialism and coloniality now make up the exhibition space, so that visitors can learn a little more about how these collections came to be in the German capital. Moreover, the 'Humboldt Forum Editorial' tries to unpack the issue

18   *No Humboldt 21! — Dekoloniale Einwände gegen das Humboldt Forum*, ed. by Mareike Heller (Berlin: AfricAvenir International, 2017).

of how Germany can come to terms with its colonial history. In the volume published in 2021, for example, the statement that connects the nine essays is 'a world in which coloniality is no longer possible'.[19] Nevertheless, these efforts are very limited and insufficient, especially given that the current cultural landscape displays tendencies for commodifying the decolonial critique itself. It becomes even more contradictory as the Humboldt Forum does not take more concrete steps regarding the efforts for restitution, and as it continues to show Benin bronzes.[20]

The opening ceremony took place on 22 September 2021. Chimamanda Ngozi Adichie made the keynote speech,[21] in which she emphasized the importance of

19 My translation of: 'eine Welt, in der Kolonialität nicht mehr möglich ist'. See David Blankenstein, Michael Dieminger, Ibou Diop, Michael Mathis, and Amel Ouaissa, 'Humboldt Forum Editorial', *Humboldt Forum Magazine*, 4 (2021) <https://www.humboldtforum.org/de/magazin/artikel/editorial-eine-welt-in-der-kolonialitaet-nicht-mehr-moeglich-ist/> [accessed 9 January 2023].

20 Benin Bronzes are a group of historical bronze sculptures including decorated cast plaques, commemorative heads, and personal ornaments. Dating back to at least the 16th century, these pieces were originally from the ancient Kingdom of Benin, in present-day Nigeria. In 1897 British forces looted these artefacts, which are still available in museums and private collections throughout Europe. At least 1,100 looted artefacts have been in Germany. The history of the acquisition of these artworks and their intrinsic connection with the colonial past has led to criticism of the exhibition of these objects in European museums. Last year, an agreement between the Preußischer Kulturbesitz and the state of Nigeria decided that one-third of the Benin Bronzes will remain on loan in Berlin for at least ten years. Recently, the Nigerian President, Muhammadu Buhari, announced that some of the artworks would be given to the Oba of Benin, Ewuare II, who is considered the original owner and custodian of the heritage and tradition of the former Kingdom of Benin. The Nigerian government has shared plans for the creation of a National Museum of Unity in Abuja.

21 Chimamanda Ngozi Adichie, 'Keynote Speech on the Occasion of the Opening of the Ethnologisches Museum and the Museum für Asiatische Kunst', video recording, Humboldt Forum Youtube Channel, 22 September 2021 <https://www.youtube.com/watch?v=gMRv5xhMCo4> [accessed 14 December 2022].

European nations confronting their role in the history of colonial violence. The museum collections are a perfect example for witnessing this violence. The Humboldt Forum alone holds today 20,000 African and Asian artefacts. Adichie drew attention to the importance of the debates on the restitution of these objects and to the fact that concrete action is needed rather than promises. Only actions, such as the return of stolen goods, can promote a reparative process in the long run. In her speech, she also reminded the audience of the value of publicly remembering these violent and violently repressed pasts.

German President Frank-Walter Steinmeier also gave a speech. He stated that although Germans are historically aware of many of the past events, when it comes to those concerning the German colonial past, there are still 'too many blanks'. His speech did not highlight German responsibility for the violence promoted during the thirty years of colonialism, nor did it highlight how Germany still benefits from its colonial legacies.

It is time to 'change our blindness towards the past'.[22] Many activists, institutions, artists, and researchers have stressed the importance of making this colonial past visible. In other words, we need to keep shedding light on the fragments that make up this entangled history. Making Germany's hidden yet omnipresent colonial past visible in official history and everyday life can also help us trace the continuity of ongoing colonial relations in the present. This is of utmost importance for the possibility of restitution, which I believe is a fundamental way of achieving the goal of decolonization.

---

22   Ibid.

Object: This Not-a-Paper 'on' the Andropobscenic University

BRUNA MARTINS COELHO

Dear nobodies,

I solemnly announce my fatigue. Hosted by a friend in President Lula's town, I am re-writing this letter, originally drafted amidst YouTube windows and inside my thirty-square-meter Greifswalder Straße apartment. The workspace was chaotic — to say the least. There were leftovers on the counter, a few duplicate files, triple stress. Organization comes later, also in this new room. Yet, there is no more Pușok meowing, interrupting me, and beating a retreat, sickened by cheap cat chow. Arriving with 600 felines after the first Russian offensive, alongside inflation and military metaphors, he remained in Berlin with my partner — again. But let me clear the counter and move the desktop windows to start this letter properly.

Christian Laval and Pierre Dardot on one side of the screen, lesser-known scholars on the other, with their YouTube speeches about the university. My Zotero's endless

folders: article, scholarship 1, 2, and 3, course 1, PhD, translation project, scientific plan, ICI Berlin paper, Deleuze
course, funding report 2, thesis, andropobscenic concept
— postponed task for... the future? The podcasts of these
brilliant, sober academic men have paradoxically put me
in a good mood. Nothing like Donna Haraway's laughter
on the Chthulucene, Paul Preciado's high heels and dildos,
Adrienne Rich's 'Politics of Location', Gloria Anzaldúa
'Letter to 3rd World Women Writers', 'Ladin Amefrican
women',[1] as Lélia Gonzalez would define those from South
America, long before the UN — and neoliberal — fabrication of the term Global South.

'What strategies do we need as researchers from the
South, situated as we are in the North?', you asked in the
call to this volume. Trying to escape from the complacency
I fear,[2] I re-write this letter, recollecting the introductory
statement of Adrienne's essay, where she announces the
multiple territorialities and anchorages of her body and

---

1   In the 1980s, Lélia Gonzalez, a black philosopher and anthropologist,
     expanded the concept of 'amefricanity' beyond national borders, en-
     compassing the narratives of black individuals and indigenous peoples
     across the Americas. She introduced the term 'Ladina Amefrica', bor-
     rowing it from a prior discussion about its origin, to denounce the
     erasure of African origins in the designation of the Latin American
     continent, which, being named this way, was associated with Latin
     European culture — what has been the effect of the historical pro-
     cess of whitening. Furthermore, her choice of the adjective 'ladino'
     instead of 'latino' in naming is the option for a signifier that, in 'pretu-
     guese' (contraction of portuguese + black [preto] diasporic languages),
     means cunning, clever, and also slave or acculturated Indian. See Lélia
     Gonzalez, 'A categoria político-cultural de amefricanidade', in *Por um
     feminismo afro-latino-americano: ensaios, intervenções e diálogos*, ed. by
     Flávia Rios and Márcia Lima (Rio de Janeiro: Zahar, 2020), pp. 127–
     38.

2   Gloria Anzaldúa, 'Letter To 3rd World Women Writers', in *This Bridge
     Called My Back: Writings by Radical Women of Color*, ed. by Cherríe
     Moraga and Gloria Anzaldúa (Watertown, MA: Persephone Press,
     1981), pp. 165–74 (p. 168).

subjectivity, expressing a certain collapse in the political
subject of feminism. A precise signifier appeared when
you asked for positioned papers: 'reduction', in reference
to the academic reception of Southern works due to the
supposed particularity of their objects, as well as to the
outcome of Eurocentric generalizations. One feeling was
also named: frustration.

LOCATION AND THE POLITICAL SUBJECT: POSITIONED I AND... US?

Rich's words laid down on paper are those 'to be spoken'
in Europe, 'having to be' sought in the US. Clarity emerges
within the instability of statements and syntax, within the
absence of a defined reader of the notes — symptomatic
of that of an identifiable political collectivity. The body
as a starting point for political reflection and epistemological action, as it was for an entire generation since the
late 1960s, didn't solve Rich's problem — it was just the
beginning. The imperative or conditional tense marking
the repeated hesitation towards what is going to be said,
and her positionality, accompany the trouble using the
pronouns 'I' and 'we', to whom Rich — and I — address
ourselves. This woman, Adrienne, who is also a Marxist
lesbian Jewish mother, 'would have' spoken as a 'feminist
"who happened" to be a white United States citizen.'[3] Dif-
fering from the no nation or homeland woman depicted
by Virginia Woolf,[4] her position is defined not through
the negation, 'I have no country | I want no country | my
country is the whole word', but, instead, by the impossibil-

---

3   Adrienne Rich, 'Notes Towards a Politics of Location', in *Blood, Bread
     and Poetry: Selected Prose 1979–1985*, ed. by Adrienne Rich (London:
     Little Brown and Co.), pp. 211–31 (p. 211).

4   Rich quotes Virginia Woolf's statement from *Three Guineas*. Cf. Ibid.

ity of fully determining the political subject she convokes. Coming from the geography of nation states to the matter of a body on the planet, writing from her paradoxically non-white whiteness, that of a Jewish body carrying in its cellular memory Nazism and the anti-communist rhetoric of the Cold War, *she can also speak* as a woman maker of theories — a white one, never raped or forcefully sterilized, and only minimally violated by the healthcare system. Listening to the black and feminist struggles and theories of the 1970s and 1980s, her theoretical-affective movement reveals, also, the scars of her body, mourning and feelings; and also, how the obsessive building of nationality through whiteness and its myths and fantasies on the origins of people, nations, families, and individuals — blood, sperm, milk — conceals the non-white constitution of an entire territory and its inhabitants.

'White eye sees from the center' — Adrienne does not entirely believe in that, but finds herself thinking so nonetheless. The recurring question, 'Who are we?', insistent in Rich's paradoxical sentence juxtaposition, 'You cannot speak for me | I cannot speak for us',[5] drives her to conclude with partial and provisional notes that I labelled, in my software, similarly to the tag applied to my *Testo Junkie* observations: 'political subject of....'.

Feminism? Anthropocene? Androcene? Metabolic rupture? 99%?

---

5   Mbembe states, in *Critique of Black Reason*, that neoliberal development increases the violence of the transformation of human populations into human-things under the reign of capital markets. He claims that for subaltern humanity racial slavery 'has now become the norm', which is independent of the centrality of racialization processes — nationalisms (and sexisms, which he does not address) function as vectors for the legitimation of the production of difference. See Achille Mbembe, *Critique de la raison nègre* (Paris: La Découverte, 2013), p. 14.

Bypassing this question, Preciado, in this bodily essay, states: 'I am not interested here in my feelings, as mine [...] but in how they are crossed [...] by that which emanates from the planet's history, from the living species' evolution, economic flows, residues of technological innovations, from the preparation of wars, the slave and merchandise trade.'[6]

If 'white eye sees from the center', I cannot stop wondering how brown are mine. Do they come from the Global South? Looking at the mirror, *saisirai-je les couleurs* of this transient gaze? Could I grasp, *en esas miradas*, the impressions of the crossings, from my *corpo lésbico* raised in a family living in a gated community (to put it simply, a gated family) to my academic education in philosophy, as a scholar, having lived — *latina* — in six different residences during the doctoral period? *Wo ist denn der Spiegel* (Where is the mirror)? Was it forgotten in Berlin, Paris, Toulouse, São Paulo... Itapevi? Did I ever *possess* it?

FRUSTRATION AND THE OTHER: REPOSITIONING
THE PROBLEM OUT OF THE HALL OF MIRRORS

As foreigners on Global North academic obstacle courses, according to our economic, cultural, symbolic, and social capital,[7] we are turned from white into non-white by our speech and gestures. Systematic institutional oblivion is translated into many forms: bureaucratic stupidity and the racist and xenophobic dysfunctionality of administrations

---

6   Paul B. Preciado, *Testo Yonqui. Sexo, Droga y Biopolítica* (Barcelona: Espasa, 2008), p. 15; my translation.

7   Cf. Pierre Bourdieu, 'Le Capital social — notes provisoires', *Actes de la recherche en sciences sociales*, 31 (1980), pp. 2–3; Pierre Bourdieu and Jean-Claude Passeron, *La Reproduction: Éléments d'une théorie du système d'enseignement* (Paris: Les Éditions de Minuit, 1970), p. 284; Pierre Bourdieu, *La Distinction: Critique sociale du jugement* (Paris: Les Éditions de Minuit, 1979).

(ignorant of the existential-territorial value of visa-related matriculation);[8] the unaccountable expenditure of hours, money, and energy with migration(s); the lack of social protection inherent to short-term labour contracts and scholarships — some of them entailing the national state's territorial right over the holder's body, supposedly to avoid brain drain.[9] We move from one residence to another, one country to the next.

I would like, though, to propose a narrative beyond the regime of identities. Rather than using the European colonizer's mirror and the optical Eurocentric metaphors *to reflect* on our identities — a major ongoing problem since the independence of our Latin American countries — let us close our eyes. As we walk through the Brandenburg Lake District, along the banks of the Seine, the Tagus, or Lake Maggiore, the images formed in these waters are different when spoken in the languages that weave our territories. Frustration on the 'North' side of the Atlantic is gold over ~~there~~ — here.

Having said this, I echo the questions posed by numerous authors. Has the identity of Southern thinkers served us, and for what? Have feminist epistemologies opened up space in the restricted universe of the human sciences? Have critical race studies accomplished the decolonization of knowledge?

Yes and no. My cat meowed — there.

---

8   Grada Kilomba, *Plantation Memories: Episodes of Everyday Racism* (Toronto: Between the Lines, 2021).

9   Some national states like Brazil have neither a policy for the hiring of PhD graduates from doctoral funding programmes abroad nor a broader understanding of possible counterparts. These PhD graduates are contractually compelled to stay on national territory for a period equivalent to that of the scholarship. Cf. Rodrigo de Oliveira Andrade, 'Retorno compulsório', *Revista Pesquisa Fapesp*, 267 (May 2018) <https://revistapesquisa.fapesp.br/retorno-compulsorio/> [accessed December 2022].

CASES OF ACADEMIC PRECARIOUSNESS

No one in my circle of PhD philosophers — Europeans and non-Europeans — aspires to a university professor position. Since the list is long, I summarize it: two Brazilian, white, middle-class heterosexual colleagues — a man and a woman — with PhD degrees, respectively, from the University of São Paulo and Humboldt University; two colleagues — white, heterosexual men — from the University of Toulouse — one Chilean, another Italian; three French colleagues, two of them *normalien.ne.s,* that is, from elite national institutions, one of whom is the daughter of one of the directors of a major French art museum. Among the PhDs from my undergraduate entourage who remained in Brazil, nobody has a permanent position at a federal university. One should consider that we were born in the eighties, an 'old' generation whose academic education lasted at least eleven years (different from the current cycles of eight years) and which has faced an expansion of the university system — its 'democratization', representing an immense creation of professor positions for colleagues of previous generations. Some results: one colleague teaches at a private high school, and two others became a shaman and a psychoanalyst. There is also a friend who is studying for the *agrégation*, another who got a two-year contract after a burnout arising from the end of her dissertation, hourly teaching contracts, and the fruitless seeking of postdoctoral positions in France, Switzerland, and Germany. Three others are constantly looking for postdocs and accumulating part-time jobs at the same time, related to academia or not. The two colleagues currently in Germany are focusing on the *Habilitation* — the first one is a straight middle-class guy with a child, unemployed, who works for free at a research institution to get rid of his scholarship debt, while the second one works part-time for the Swiss press.

As I can no longer believe that it is out of love for knowledge or compulsion to repeat that we work on weekends or
during vacations; nor that we answer institutional emails at
11:30 p.m. due to obsessive neurosis... Since good-girl behaviour or a people-pleasing character does not explain why
scholars renounce parenting in the name of science; nor
can Stockholm syndrome explain donating our work for
the collective good... Given that the death drive cannot account for the risk of unemployment after twenty academic
years, it is *healthy* to consider the structural *raison d'être*
of this culture of suffering. Its macroeconomic logic and
micropolitics are neoliberalism on one side, and the university caste system on the other. #Foucault and Bourdieu.

THE BRAZILIAN STRUCTURAL FRACTURE OF THE WORLD: NOT WORKERS, BUT LABOURING NOMADS

The 'Becoming Black of the World' and the 'Brazilization'
or 'favelization' of the world are concepts created to grasp
a peculiar neoliberal *feitiço*: the universalization of misery, through the very same mechanisms in the Global
South and North. Thanks to the work of capital, racial
slavery would have 'now become the norm' for subaltern
humanity, according to Cameroonian philosopher Achille
Mbembe in 2013. This phrase might establish a dialogue
with the diagnosis on the Brazilianization of the world,
whose genealogy was established by Brazilian Marxist philosopher Paulo Arantes in 2004. Emerging in the 1990s
from the pen of German sociologist Ulrich Beck and US
thinkers,[10] who were stunned by the outcome of neoliberalism's final victory, this term described the mutation

---

10   Among these intellectuals are Edward Luttwak, Michael Lind, Christopher Lasch, and Richard Rorty. Cf. Paulo Arantes, *A fratura brasileira
do mundo: visões do laboratório brasileiro da mundialização* (São Paulo:
Editora 34, 2001).

in labour relations and financialization-derived phenomena: the alternation between formal and informal labour cycles, the shrinking of the middle classes, the impoverishment of racialized and female populations, social immobility, general insecurity, and the escalation of state violence against its populations, which were once common in the Global South, landed in the North. The devouring dispossession machine of capitalist accumulation, which, despite being defined as 'primitive', has stubbornly persisted as a historical condition of modernity and 'post'-modernity (industrial progress, *welfare states*, and citizenship in the 'North'), produces, through intensified financial capital valorization independent of human labour, hungry, homeless, non-integrable populations. Living in the dumps or in *favelas*, they are reduced to the condition of social garbage described by Lélia Gonzalez in the 1970s, or of the enslaved whose body becomes 'plant, and stone, and mud, and nothing', as once wrote one of the greatest black literary portraitists of slaveholding Brazil, Machado de Assis. If raciality thus produces the 'other of Europe' as a being without determination,[11] as Denise Ferreira da Silva and Paula Chakravartty described, this condition was that of the proletarian as a generic being described by Marx. 'The proletarian is without property', he writes in 'Manifesto of Communist Party', and proceeds:

> His relation to his wife and children has no longer anything in common with the bourgeois family relations; modern industry labour, modern subjection to capital, the same in England as in France, in America as in Germany, has stripped him of every

---

11   Paula Chakravartty and Denise Ferreira da Silva, 'Accumulation, Dispossession, and Debt: The Racial Logic of Global Capitalism — An Introduction', *American Quarterly*, 64.3 (September 2012), pp. 361–85 (p. 369).

> trace of national character. Law, morality, religion,
> are to him so many bourgeois prejudices, behind
> which lurk in ambush just as many bourgeois inter-
> ests.[12]

Devoid of identifying predicates that correspond to social recognition signs, this proletarian condition would translate the exact measure of his material dispossession (which was not however thought by Marx in its violently gendered character, the dispossession proper to reproductive labour and rape).

Another day, reading *The Guardian*, I felt sorry. A woman teaching at the University of London lives in a tent[13]. The difficulties she has dressing properly to teach and dealing with the winter as a problem do not exist for the small sedentary caste of her colleagues. Nomadism, minimalism, Kindle, long-distance relationships are the portrait of the migrant intellectualized middle class, disgracefully chic. Docile, silent, and governable, we accept a form of exploitation that would be experienced with indignation by other professional sectors.

MANAGERIAL PROTESTANTISM AGAINST THE WELFARE STATE 'PARASITES': MAKING KNOWLEDGE-*PHILIA* PROFITABLE

The university worldwide has been dismantled, but not by the ones often accused of interfering with its structure. Obtaining a permanent position is a governmentally produced delusion, if we consider some simultaneous processes and

---

12   Karl Marx and Frederick Engels, 'Manifesto of the Communist Party', in *Marx/Engels Selected Works*, ed. by Engels (Moscow: Progress Publishers, 1969), pp. 98–137 (p. 20).

13   Anna Fazackerley, '"My Students Never Knew": The Lecturer Who Lived in a Tent', *The Guardian*, 30 October 2021,<https://www.theguardian.com/education/2021/oct/30/my-students-never-knew-the-lecturer-who-lived-in-a-tent> [accessed 3 December 2022].

logics. Safeguarding local and genealogical specificities, they follow general — neoliberal — lines of precariza-tion,[14] and consist in the 'democratization' of access to education carried out since the early 2000s (that also represented the elitism of universities translated into the seals of excellence) and the maintenance of the caste-like university system. Wholeheartedly hoping that this statement was inaccurate, that it was just a bad day, premenstrual tension, or saturnine pessimism, I rapidly looked at some numbers underlying the neoliberal culture of academic suffering.

In Germany, only 12% of the academic staff is offered a permanent position after *Habilitation* and scholars often emigrate due to lack of prospects.[15] The expansion of university education coincided with increased competition between institutions due to the predominantly public (80%)

---

14   We draw from the conceptions of Ruy Braga and Giovanni Alves, for whom the precariat is a social layer of the proletarian class, not a new social class. Cf. Ruy Braga, *A política do precariado: do populismo à hegemonia lulista* (São Paulo: Boitempo, 2012); Giovanni Alves, *Trabalho e subjetividade: o espírito do toyotismo na era do capitalismo manipulatório* (São Paulo: Boitempo, 2010).

15   Kolja Lindner arrives at these figures about the composition of university professors and researchers from the numbers provided by the conference of university presidents in 2017. According to Lindner's analyses of the 'Gutachten zu Forschung, Innovation und Technologischer Leistungsfähigkeit Deutschlands' (2014) and the 'Statistische Daten und Forschungsbefunde zu Promovierenden und Promovierten in Deutschland' (2018), between 1996 and 2011, 4,000 more departures than arrivals occurred. Between 2001 and 2010, the emigration rate of teacher-researchers was 13%. In 2010, 54% of teacher-researchers in the humanities and 48% of those in the social sciences declared their willingness to emigrate to find a position. Cf. Kolja Lindner, 'Le Modèle allemand: précarité et résistances dans l'enseignement supérieur et la recherche d'outre-Rhin', in *Liberté de la recherche. Conflits, pratiques, horizons*, ed. by Mélanie Duclos and Anders Fjeld (Paris: Editions Kimäe, 2019), pp. 209–18, available online <https://shs.hal.science/halshs-02496377/document> [accessed 5 October 2023], pp. 1–6 (pp. 1–2).

Drittmittel funding, which has enabled the winners in the race for funds to create graduate schools and *Exzellenzclusters*, has forbidden the establishment of full professorships, and has promoted short-term contracts. This explains why, among the 'rest' of staff, 38% are temporary (385,311 people), 50% of which hold contracts of barely one year.[16] The prospect of a permanent position is but a fantasy for those who, recruited as *Studentassistenz*, are counted on the payroll of Berlin universities in the same way as furniture and utensils; for those who, hired as *Lehrkraft für besondere Aufgabe* (lecturer with special responsibilities), provide teaching at the expense of their own education; for those who, as *Wissenschaftliche Mitarbeiter*in* (scientific assistant), accumulate postdoctoral fellowships and short-term contracts for up to six years;[17] for those who, as *Privatdozent*in* (Adjunct Professor), having passed the *Habilitation*, are still *selbstständig* (self-employed). Each survivor of the long ordeal to Habilitation, who is one of among 10,000 people with privilege in terms of symbolic, cultural, and economic capital,[18] intimately related to their

---

16   Ibid, p. 1.

17   This temporal limitation to hiring on a fixed-term contract in public service after the doctorate (and to six years of fixed-term contract before the doctorate) stems, according to Kolja Lindner, from the law *Wissenschaftszeitvertragsgesetz* (2007) (similar to the Sauvadet French law (2012)). Relying on the 'Hochschulen in Zahlen 2017', he shows that this law favours then-precarious modes of financing such as scholarships or vacations. Only third-party funding (public or private, which in 2017 accounted for 15% of the budget of the university system) is an exception to this rule. Cf. Ibid, p. 2.

18   Following Lindner's analysis and sources, I arrived at this approximate number considering that, in 2019, 6,609 people were in this situation and the average annual rise of the holders of Habilitation is 1,677. Cf. Statistisches Bundesamt, 'Personal an Hochschulen 2016', p. 37 <https://www.destatis.de/DE/Themen/Gesellschaft-Umwelt/Bildung-Forschung-Kultur/Hochschulen/Publikationen/Downloads-Hochschulen/personal-vorbericht-5213402168004.pdf?__blob=publicationFile> [accessed 15 December 2022] and

'race', gender, sexuality, age, and ability, will have to beat another four equally qualified people.[19] Other factors exacerbate this fragile work situation: the loss of other social rights; the tiny number of union members in universities, contrasting with the 60% increase in membership for workers in other categories; the intransigence of the German state in negotiations with social movements opposed to academic precariousness; the small numerical importance of activists and the timidity of their demands.[20] The Association of the Chancellors of the Universities of Germany justified the predominance of temporary employment contracts, presumably to create the needed vacancies for the future generation. The precarious staff is thus villainized for its claims against short-term contracts. If the demands of this class were heeded, it 'would paralyse the continuous promotion of young scientists and thus undermine this special function of the science system and indirectly further exacerbate the shortage of skilled workers in the economy and society'.[21]

Statistisches Bundesamt, 'Zahl der Habilitationen 2017 gegenüber Vorjahr geringfügig um 0,3 % gestiegen' <https://www.destatis.de/DE/Presse/Pressemitteilungen/2018/07/PD18_242_213.html> [accessed 15 December 2022].

19 Cf. Nicolas Pons-Vignon, 'Reflections on the Paradox of German Academic Precarity' (Kassel: ICDD, University of Kassel), online video recording, YouTube, 17 December 2019 <https://www.youtube.com/watch?v=c4TMikEHMr4> [accessed 15 December 2022].

20 TVStud's demands were, according to Lindner, timid: recognition as workers, not as furniture, and inflationary replacement. Mentioning the other movements created after 2016 (unter_bau13, Netzwerk für gute Arbeit in der Wissenschaft (NgAWiss), and Uni Kassel Unbefristet), he highlighted the little effect these demands had on political mobilization, based as they were on trade union negotiations typical of the German corporatist culture (priority being given to negotiations rather than to mobilization). Cf. Lindner, p. 5.

21 Vereinigung der Kanzlerinnen und Kanzler der Universitäten Deutschlands, 'Bayreuther Erklärung zu befristeten Beschäftigungsverhältnissen mit wissenschaftlichem und künstlerischem

In France, the university also works through massive exploitation of precarious workers. 40% of non-tenured staff are responsible for administrative work, 70% of undergraduate teachers are precarious — officially paid below the minimum wage — and research is partly based on social assistance (Revenu de Solidarité Active, unemployment insurance, or undeclared work).[22]

In Brazil, university precarization affects professors in the public and private sectors. Professionals hired in private institutions — the largest part of the labour market (54%), owned by business groups that explore the expanding market of diplomas[23] — are submitted to superexploitative working conditions: required to ensure the instruction of different subjects in several courses — that is, unpaid working hours in developing new subjects — they also perform administrative tasks and are underpaid. More expensive professionals holding doctoral degrees are forced to resign. In the public service, precarization becomes the norm: the number of public competitions for professor positions has decreased; temporary hiring — as substitute lecturers deprived of rights — becomes a common practice adopted in several public institutions, federal and provincial.[24] In addition, the reduction of pub-

Personal in Universitäten', September 2019 <https://www.uni-kanzler.de/fileadmin/user_upload/05_Publikationen/2017_-_2010/20190919_Bayreuther_Erklaerung_der_Universitaetskanzler_final.pdf> [accessed 15 December 2022].

22   Cf. Université Ouverte, 'La Précarité dans l'enseignement et la recherche', 10 February 2020 <https://universiteouverte.org/2020/02/10/la-precarite-dans-lenseignement-et-la-recherche/> [accessed 15 May 2023].

23   Instituto Nacional de Estudos e Pesquisas Educacionais Anísio Teixeira, Censo da Educação superior — Notas Estatísticas — 2019 (Brasília: Ministério da Educação, 2019), p. 25.

24   Antonio de Paula Bosi, 'A precarização do trabalho docente nas instituições de ensino superior do Brasil nesses últimos 25 anos', Educação & Sociedade, 28.101 (2007), p. 1503–23.

lic investments in those institutions has meant increased pressure on professors and researchers, who are in charge of raising funds with private and public powers, and who, to this end, must produce knowledge and publish according to the productivity standards imposed by regulatory agencies.

Scholars, as a class, do not protest enough against precariousness. The effects of this perpetual race for funds on all academic levels includes time spent responding to calls for proposals and bureaucratic procedures; the material, symbolic, and pedagogical dependencies on the professor; professorships being transformed into managerial positions; and the constitution of an academic *habitus* and a self-entrepreneurial subjectivation that obstructs, both within and beyond the universities, collective action, solidarity, and collaboration between researchers. The fantasy of becoming a professor and, thus, the need to please the holders of this position due to its rarity… all this devotion to the ethics of capitalism and neoliberal rationality points to desire[25] — this is the astuteness of neoliberal ideology, unconscious suicidal servitude, and full occupation. #Dardot+Laval.

---

25 Christian Laval and Pierre Dardot seek to understand neoliberal governance within a broader reflection on neoliberalism and the role of the university in the dynamics of neoliberal subject production, whose figure is that of the entrepreneur. They describe how the subjective logic of desire is inscribed onto the logics and mechanisms of the accumulation of capital, marked by the ideology of professionalization, competition, and innovation that is characteristic of a corporate culture present in European educational establishments since kindergarten. Christian Laval and Pierre Dardot, 'Grande conférence (FQPPU)', online video recording, YouTube, 2017 <https://www.youtube.com/watch?v=LGFpK3LJGGk> [accessed 15 December 2022]. Cf. Pierre Dardot and Christian Laval, *La Nouvelle Raison du monde: essai sur la société néolibérale* (Paris: La Découverte, 2010).

CAPITAL'S CAPTURE OF MINORITY AGENDAS
THROUGH LABELLING

Historically, there have been many feminist, black, decolonial, Marxist, anti-capitalist people struggling for the recognition of other epistemologies and corporealities and denouncing the productive and reproductive artificiality of the distinctions between domestic and public, the logic and effects of necroliberalism,[26] and the regime of commodification and minorization of knowledge. One of our greatest enemies is the delegation of our critical potential to the private initiative. The market — sustainable, humanitarian, and sometimes 'angry' — functions as the only Subject through the creation of diversity and green labels, the appropriation of languages of empowerment and social justice tied to the image of an economy run by black people, women, and queer people.[27] The dissemination of this imaginary accompanies the political silencing around quotas. Glass ceilings or leaky pipelines remain untouched

---

26   Elsa Dorlin has forged this concept in dialogue with Achille Mbembe's theorization of necropolitics and necroeconomics, the concept of the state of exception, and Foucault's reflections on fascism. Cf. Elsa Dorlin, 'Démocratie suicidaire', *Esprit*, 12 (2018) <https://esprit.presse.fr/article/elsa-dorlin/democratie-suicidaire-41832> [accessed 15 December 2022].

27   Sirma Bilge points out how the logic of knowledge production about intersectionality benefits white researchers and contributes to the erasure of the authors that posed the problems of the crossing of the forms of domination from the 1970s. See Sirma Bilge, 'Le Blanchiment de l'intersectionnalité', *Recherches feministes*, 28.2 (2015), pp. 9–32. Since the 1970s, theorists of neoliberalism like Gilles Deleuze and Felix Guattari from one side, and Michel Foucault from another, aiming to overcome the rigidity of structural diagnoses in the Communist Party and the risks of fascistization within leftist movements, have depicted, respectively, how the capitalist schizophrenic and schizophrenia-inducing machine converts everyone and everything into exploitable capital through identification, counting, registering; and how social control also produces the resistances and language of struggles.

in the North, as in the South. In German academia, women, whose representation has increased a timid 8% in ten years (15% to 23% from 2005 to 2015),[28] are 32% less likely to follow a career path leading to a professorship, corresponding in 2019 to 31% of those with *Habilitation* and 26% of full professors.[29] Considering the state and academic hegemonic categories used for surveys, women seem to have neither colour nor nationality, all possessing, as natural entities, the same straight pink vaginas. As for the Brazilian or French data, would it be naïve to imagine that they are similar to the German data?

Profitable diversity is the well-behaved, whitewashed version found in organic shops or greenmarkets, while so-called mother nature is collapsing, representing a risk to the not-so-*sapiens* species (although the intensity of damage is unequally distributed).[30] In the context of the world crisis of representative democracy and the transformation of nation states into managers of the best scenario for the multiplication of finance, precarious living conditions, excessive work, increasing individualism, and the lack of class consciousness lead a substantial portion of the critical mass to lose spaces in which the common can be constructed — the university itself, unions, collectives. This is in the event that the critical mass aren't purely and simply co-opted by companies whose highly qualified workforce is

---

28 Cf. Pons-Vignon, 'Reflections on the Paradox of German Academic Precarity'.

29 Katrin Heinrichs and Hendrik Sonnabend, 'Leaky Pipeline or Glass Ceiling? Empirical Evidence from the German Academic Career Ladder', *Applied Economics Letters*, 2 (2022), pp. 1–5.

30 Fernanda Rosário, Letícia Filho, and Victor Oliveira, 'O perfil da COP-26 mostra que o debate sobre o clima ainda exclui as mulheres', *Alma preta*, 3 September 2022 <https://almapreta.com.br/sessao/politica/so-macho-perfil-da-cop-mostra-que-o-debate-climatico-ainda-exclui-mulheres/> [accessed 15 December 2022].

available at the lowest cost in universities, which also function as a publicity platform and consumer market. The environment — in crisis — does not escape from neoliberal governance and green coloniality: nature, already transformed into commodities, becomes a 'supplier of services', of carbon markets and assets linked to the Earth's genetic codes listed in Amazonia.[31] Thanks to the energetic alliance established between Germany and Brazil, the latter country will furnish energy that will guarantee the neutrality of European carbon emissions until 2050. Germany there sees an opportunity: low-cost green hydrogen from Brazil would allow it to decarbonize its steel mills after equipping the tropical country with photovoltaic and wind energy machines and establishing partnerships.

Many scientists indirectly play on the team of the mad tycoons on duty, with their colonial delirium of infinite progress, of zero-waste and no-loss technologies. In this financialized Andropobscene capitalism, in which environmental catastrophes, crises, and wars become opportunities for those who intend to make the universe their families' corner, we cannot let technocracy impose itself as the only response to the fear of the fears: the extinction not of the *species*, but of utopias.

I wonder if it is suitable and desirable to seek to affirm our place as Southern researchers in this structure, weaving not-so-offensive micropolitical corrosive strategies.

---

31   Cf. Michael Schmidlehner, 'Banco de Códigos da Amazônia', in *Uwa'Kürü: dicionário analítico*, ed. by Gerson de Albuquerque and Agenor Pacheco (Rio Branco: Edufac & Nepan Editora, 2020), pp. 28–37.

A poem, then.

> We aren't in the bush to clear a path, nor are we ants.
> Suddenly it dawned on us: our machete is a penknife.
> Seeds cannot grow in a minefield;
> here, we do something else.
>
> *I'm Nobody! Who are you?*
> We are many, no less.
>
> It is not harvest time.
> Hope and despair are useless to build houses.
> Second World War bombs still explode.
> We dwell inside them.
>
> *Are you — Nobody — too?*
>
> We are
> not the same.
>
> Exactly
> in this place.
>
> *Don't tell! they'd advertise — you know! How dreary — to*
> *   be — Somebody!*
>
> One courage
> upon
> another.
>
> It urges to be being.
> We are
> no buts.

With love,

   B.

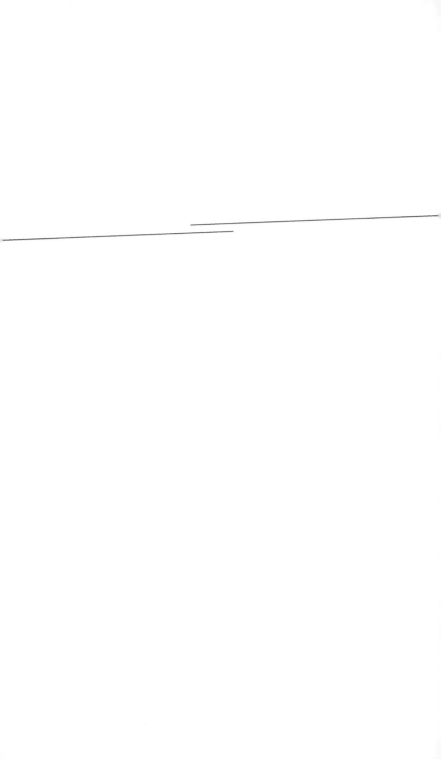

References

Abungu, George Okello, 'Die Frage nach Restitution und Rückgabe: Ein Dialog der Interessen', in *(Post)Kolonialismus und Kulturelles Erbe: Internationale Debatten im Humboldt Forum*, ed. by Dortje Fink and Martina Urioste-Buschmann (Munich: Hanser, 2021), pp. 110–31

Adichie, Chimamanda Ngozi, 'Keynote Speech on the Occasion of the Opening of the Ethnologisches Museum and the Museum für Asiatische Kunst', video recording, Humboldt Forum Youtube Channel, 22 September 2021 <https://www.youtube.com/watch?v=gMRv5xhMCo4> [accessed 14 December 2022]

Adorno, Theodor W., *Minima Moralia: Reflections on a Damaged Life*, trans. by E. F. N. Jephcott, Radical Thinkers (London: Verso, 2005)

Ahmed, Sara, *The Feminist Killjoy Handbook* (London: Allen Lane, 2023)

—— *Living a Feminist Life* (Durham, NC: Duke University Press, 2017)

Aitken, Robbie, 'The First German Colonial Exhibition (1896)', Black Central Europe Studies Network (BCESN) <https://blackcentraleurope.com/sources/1850-1914/the-first-german-colonial-exhibition-1896/> [accessed 2 January 2023]

Alatas, Syed Farid, 'Religion and Concept Formation: Transcending Eurocentrism', in *Eurocentrism at the Margins*, ed. by Lutfi Sunar (New York: Routledge, 2016), pp. 87–102

Althusser, Louis, *For Marx*, trans. by Ben Brewster (London: Verso, 2005)

—— *Montesquieu: la politique et l'histoire* (Paris: PUF, 1992)

Althusser, Louis, and others, *Reading Capital*, trans. by Ben Brewster and David Fernbach (London: Verso, 2015)

Alves, Giovanni, *Trabalho e subjetividade: o espírito do toyotismo na era do capitalismo manipulatório* (São Paulo: Boitempo, 2010)

Amanat, Abbas, *Iran: A Modern History* (New Haven, CT: Yale University Press, 2017)

Amanat, Abbas, and Assef Ashraf, eds, *The Persianate World: Rethinking a Shared Sphere* (Leiden: Brill, 2018)

Andrade, Oswald de, 'Cannibalist Manifesto', trans. by Leslie Bary, *Latin American Literary Review*, 19.38 (1991), pp. 38–47 <https://www.jstor.org/stable/20119601>

Andrade, Rodrigo de Oliveira, 'Retorno compulsório', *Revista Pesquisa Fapesp*, 267 (May 2018) <https://revistapesquisa.fapesp.br/retorno-compulsorio/> [accessed December 2022]

Anzaldúa, Gloria, *Borderlands/La Frontera: The New Mestiza* (San Francisco, CA: Aunt Lute Books, 2012)

—— 'Letter To 3rd World Women Writers', in *This Bridge Called My Back: Writings by Radical Women of Color,* ed. by Cherríe Moraga and Gloria Anzaldúa (Watertown, MA: Persephone Press, 1981), pp. 165–74

Arantes, Paulo, *A fratura brasileira do mundo: visões do laboratório brasileiro da mundialização* (São Paulo: Editora 34, 2001)

—— *Sentimento da dialética na experiência intelectual brasileira. Dialética e dualidade segundo Antonio Cândido e Roberto Schwarz* (São Paulo: Paz e Terra, 1992)

—— *Um departamento francês de ultramar* (Rio de Janeiro: Paz e Terra, 1994)

Arjomand, Said Amir, 'A Decade of Persianate Studies', *Journal of Persianate Studies*, 8.2 (2015), pp. 309–33

—— 'From the Editor: Defining Persianate Studies', *Journal of Persianate Studies*, 1.1 (2008), pp. 1–4

—— 'Multiple Modernities and the Promise of Comparative Sociology', in *Worlds of Difference*, ed. by Said Amir Arjomand and Elisa P. Reis (London: Sage, 2013), pp. 15–39

Armiero, Marco, 'Is There an Indigenous Knowledge in the Global North? Re/Inventing Local Knowledge and Communities in the Struggles over Garbage and Incinerators in Campania, Italy', *Estudos de Sociologia*, 1.20 (2014) <https://periodicos.ufpe.br/revistas/revsocio/article/view/235511> [accessed 16 September 2022]

Ashraf, Assef, 'Introduction: Pathways to the Persianate', in Amanat and Ashraf, *The Persianate World*, pp. 1–14

Bachelard, Gaston, *La Terre et les rêveries du repos* (Paris: Librairie José Corti, 1982)

Barad, Karen, 'Posthumanist Performativity: Toward an Understanding of How Matter Comes to Matter', *Signs: Journal of Women in Culture and Society*, 28.3 (2003), pp. 801–31 <https://doi.org/10.1086/345321>

Bayat, Asef, *Life as Politics: How Ordinary People Change the Middle East* (Redwood City, CA: Stanford University Press, 2013)

Becker, Alton, *Beyond Translation: Essays toward a Modern Philology* (Ann Arbor: University of Michigan Press, 1995)

Bennabi, Malek, *Islam in History and Society*, trans. by Ashma Rashid (New Dehli: Kitabbhavan, 1999)

Berlin Biennale for Contemporary Art, 'About the 12th Berlin Biennale for Contemporary Art', website, 2022 <https://12.berlinbiennale.de/about/> [accessed 23 January 2023]

Bezirksamt Mitte: Fachbereich Kunst, Kultur und Geschichte, 'Informationen rund um die Straßenumbenennungen im Afrikanischen Viertel im Wedding, Berlin-Mitte' <https://www.berlin.de/kunst-und-kultur-mitte/geschichte/afrikanisches-viertel-609903.php> [accessed 10 January 2023]

Bilge, Sirma, 'Le Blanchiment de l'intersectionnalité', *Recherches féministes*, 28.2 (2015), pp. 9–32

Birman, Joel, 'O negro no discurso psiquiátrico', in *Cativeiro e liberdade*, ed. by Jaime da Silva et al. (Rio de Janeiro: UERJ, 1989), pp. 44–58

Blankenstein, David, and Michael Dieminger, Ibou Diop, Michael Mathis, and Amel Ouaissa, 'Humboldt Forum Editorial', *Humboldt Forum Magazine*, 4 (2021) <https://www.humboldtforum.org/de/magazin/artikel/editorial-eine-welt-in-der-kolonialitaet-nicht-mehr-moeglich-ist/> [accessed 9 January 2023]

Boccagni, Paolo, 'Homing: A Category for Research on Space Appropriation and "Home-Oriented" Mobilities', *Mobilities*, 17.4 (2022), pp. 585–601 <https://doi.org/10.1080/17450101.2022.2046977>

Bosi, Antonio de Paula, 'A precarização do trabalho docente nas instituições de ensino superior do Brasil nesses últimos 25 anos', *Educação & Sociedade*, 28.101 (2007), p. 1503–23

Bourdieu, Pierre, 'Le Capital social — notes provisoires', *Actes de la recherche en sciences sociales*, 31 (1980), pp. 2–3

—— *La Distinction: Critique sociale du jugement* (Paris: Les Éditions de Minuit, 1979)

Bourdieu, Pierre, and Jean-Claude Passeron, *La Reproduction: Éléments d'une théorie du système d'enseignement* (Paris: Les Éditions de Minuit, 1970)

Braga, Ruy, *A política do precariado: do populismo à hegemonia lulista* (São Paulo: Boitempo, 2012)

Brown, Nicholas, 'Roberto Schwarz: Mimesis Beyond Realism', in *The SAGE Handbook of Frankfurt School Critical Theory*, ed. by Beverley Best, Werner Bonefeld, and Chris O'Kane, 3 vols (Los Angeles: SAGE, 2018), I, pp. 465–78

Bruck, Gabriele vom, and Barbara Bodenhorn, *An Anthropology of Names and Naming* (Cambridge: Cambridge University Press, 2009)

Burke, Peter, *What is the History of Knowledge?* (Oxford: Polity Press, 2015)

Burns, Rob, 'Images of Alterity: Second-Generation Turks in the Federal Republic', *The Modern Language Review*, 94.3 (1999), pp. 744–57 <https://doi.org/10.2307/3736999>

Butler, Judith, *Excitable Speech: A Politics of the Performative* (New York: Routledge, 1997)

Cabañas, Kaira, *Learning from Madness: Brazilian Modernism and Global Contemporary Art* (Chicago: The University of Chicago Press, 2018)

Cardoso, Fernando Henrique, *Capitalismo e escravidão no Brasil meridional: o negro na sociedade escravocrata do Rio Grande do Sul*, 5th edn (Rio de Janeiro: Civilização Brasileira, 2003)

—— *Política e desenvolvimento em sociedades dependentes: ideologias do empresariado industrial argentino e brasileiro* (Rio de Janeiro: Zahar, 1971)

—— 'Prefácio à 2ª edição', in *Capitalismo e escravidão no Brasil meridional*, 5th edn (Rio de Janeiro: Civilização Brasileira, 2003), pp. 15–24

Carvalho, Flávio de, 'A única arte que presta é a arte anormal', in *Diário de S. Paulo* (24 September 1936), Documents of Latin American and Latino Art, International Center for the Arts of the Americas, Museum of Fine Arts, Houston <https://icaa.mfah.org/s/en/item/1084943> [accessed 20 September 2023]

Chakrabarty, Dipesh, 'Whose Anthropocene? A Response', in *Whose Anthropocene? Revisiting Dipesh Chakrabarty's 'Four Theses'*, ed. by Robert Emmett and Thomas Lekan (Munich: RCC Perspectives, 2016), pp. 103–14

Chakravartty, Paula, and Denise Ferreira da Silva, 'Accumulation, Dispossession, and Debt: The Racial Logic of Global Capitalism — An Introduction', *American Quarterly*, 64.3 (September 2012), pp. 361–85

Clot, Yves, *Éthique et travail collectif. Controverses* (Toulouse: Érès, 2020)

Coletta, Michela, 'A World without Objects: Epistemic Bordering for a Transformative Future', *FORMA — A Journal of Latin American Criticism & Theory*, 2.1 (2023), pp. 109–31

Coletta, Michela, and Malayna Raftopoulos, 'Counter-Hegemonic Narratives and the Politics of Plurality: Problematising Global Environmental Governance from Latin America through the Case of Bolivia', *Iberoamericana — Nordic Journal of Latin American and Caribbean Studies*, 47.1 (2018), pp. 108–17 <https://doi.org/10.16993/iberoamericana.429>

Collins, Patricia Hill, *Black Feminist Thought: Knowledge, Consciousness, and the Politics of Empowerment* (Boston: Hyman, 1990)

Comaroff, John, and Jean Comaroff, *Of Revelation and Revolution: The Dialectics of Modernity on a South African Frontier* (Chicago: The University of Chicago Press, 1997)

Conrad, Sebastian, 'Rethinking German Colonialism in a Global Age', *The Journal of Imperial and Commonwealth History*, 41 (2013), pp. 543–66 <https://doi.org/10.1080/03086534.2013.836352>

Costa, Elsa, '"But I Want the Truth!" The Legacy of Martial Gueroult in São Paulo Philosophy, 1935–2018', *A Contracorriente: Una revista de estudios latinoamericanos*, 18.3 (2021), pp. 70–105

Costabile-Heming, Carol Anne, 'The Reconstructed City Palace and Humboldt Forum in Berlin: Restoring Architectural Identity or Distorting the Memory of Historic Spaces?', *Journal of Contemporary European Studies*, 25 (2017), pp. 441–54

Crenshaw, Kimberle, 'Mapping the Margins: Intersectionality, Identity Politics, and Violence Against Women of Color', *Stanford Law Review*, 43.6 (1991), pp. 1241–99

Dabashi, Hamid, *The Arab Spring: The End of Postcolonialism* (London: Bloomsbury Publishing, 2012)

—— *Can Non-Europeans Think?* With a foreword by Walter Mignolo (London: Zed Books, 2015)

—— *Iran without Borders: Towards a Critique of the Postcolonial Nation* (London: Verso Books, 2016)

Dardot, Pierre, and Christian Laval, *La Nouvelle Raison du monde: essai sur la société néolibérale* (Paris: La Découverte, 2010)

Davis, Angela, *Women, Race and Class* (New York: Random House, 1981)

Dekoloniale Memory Culture in the City, 'Über uns', website <https://www.dekoloniale.de/de/about> [accessed 2 January 2023]

Delgado, L. Elena, Rolando J. Romero, and Walter Mignolo, 'Local Histories and Global Designs: An Interview with Walter Mignolo', *Discourse*, 22.3 (2000), pp. 7–33 <https://doi.org/10.1353/dis.2000.0004>

Deligny, Fernand, *Camering: Fernand Deligny on Cinema and the Image*, ed. by Marlon Miguel (Leiden: LUP, 2022)

Derrida, Jacques, 'Des tours de Babel', trans. by Joseph F. Graham, in *Difference in Translation*, ed. by Joseph Graham (Ithaca, NY: Cornell University Press, 1985), pp. 165–207

—— 'Plato's Pharmacy', in *Dissemination*, trans. by Barbara Johnson (Chicago: University of Chicago Press, 1981), pp. 61–171

Dirlik, Arif, 'Global South: Predicament and Promise', *The Global South*, 1.1 (2007), pp. 12–23

Dorlin, Elsa, 'Démocratie suicidaire', *Esprit*, 12 (2018) <https://esprit.presse.fr/article/elsa-dorlin/democratie-suicidaire-41832> [accessed 15 December 2022]

Dulley, Iracema, 'The Case and the Signifier: Generalization in Freud's Rat Man', in *The Case for Reduction*, ed. by Christoph F. E. Holzhey and Jakob Schillinger (Berlin: ICI Berlin Press, 2022), pp. 13–37

—— 'Chronicles of Bailundo: A Fragmentary Account in Umbundu of Life before and after Portuguese Colonial Rule', *Africa*, 91.5 (2021), pp. 713–41

—— 'Naming Others: Translation and Subject Constitution in the Central Highlands of Angola (1926–1961)', *Comparative Studies in Society and History*, 64.2 (2022), pp. 363–93

—— *On the Emic Gesture: Difference and Ethnography in Roy Wagner* (London: Routledge, 2019)

—— 'The Voice in Rape', *European Journal of Psychoanalysis*, 9.2 (2022) <https://www.journal-psychoanalysis.eu/articles/the-voice-in-rape/>

Dulley, Iracema, and Lorena de Avelar Muniagurria, 'Performance, processos de diferenciação e constituição de sujeitos', *R@U*, 12.1 (2020), pp. 8–18

Dussel, Enrique D., 'Europe, Modernity, and Eurocentrism', trans. by Javier Krauel and Virginia C. Tuma, *Nepantla: Views from South*, 1.3 (2000), pp. 465–78

Eisenstadt, Shmuel Noah, *Comparative Civilizations and Multiple Modernities* (Leiden: Brill, 2003)

—— 'Multiple Modernities', *Daedalus*, 129.1 (2000), pp. 1–29

El-Tayeb, Fatima, 'The Universal Museum: How the New Germany Built its Future on Colonial Amnesia', *Nka: Journal of Contemporary African Art*, 46 (2020), pp. 72–82.

Fanon, Frantz, *Alienation and Freedom*, ed. by Jean Khalfa and Robert J. C. Young, trans. by Steven Corcoran (London: Bloomsbury, 2018)

—— 'Day Hospitalization in Psychiatry: Value and Limits. Part Two: — Doctrinal Considerations', in Fanon, *Alienation and Freedom*, pp. 495–510

—— 'Letter to the Resident Minister', in Fanon, *Alienation and Freedom*, pp. 433–35

—— 'The Meeting between Society and Psychiatry', in Fanon, *Alienation and Freedom*, pp. 511–30

—— 'Mental Alterations, Character Modifications, Psychic Disorders and Intellectual Deficit in Spinocerebellar Heredodegeneration: A Case of Friedreich's Ataxia with Delusions of Possession', in Fanon, *Alienation and Freedom*, pp. 203–76

—— *Black Skin, White Masks* [1952], trans. by Charles Lam Markmann (New York: Pluto Press, 1986)

—— *The Wretched of the Earth*, trans. by Richard Philcox (New York: Grove Press, 2004)

Ferdinand, Malcolm, *Decolonial Ecology: Thinking from the Carib-bean World*, trans. by Anthony Paul Smith (Cambridge: Polity Press, 2022)

Ferreira da Silva, Denise, '1 (Life) ÷ 0 (Blackness) = ∞ − ∞ or ∞ / ∞: On Matter Beyond the Equation of Value', *E-Flux Journal*, 79 (2017) <http://worker01.e-flux.com/pdf/article_94686.pdf> [accessed 13 August 2023]

Foucault, Michel, *L'Archéologie du savoir* (Paris: Gallimard, 1969)

Franco, Maria Sylvia de Carvalho, *Homens livres na ordem escravocrata*, 4th edn (São Paulo: UNESP, 1983)

Frank, Andre Gunder, *Capitalism and Underdevelopment in Latin America: Historical Studies of Chile and Brazil* (New York: Monthly Review Press, 1967)

Giannotti, José Arthur, 'Contra Althusser', in *Exercícios de filosofia* (Petrópolis: Vozes, 1980), pp. 85–102

—— 'Entrevista com José Arthur Giannotti', *Trans/Form/Ação*, 1 (1974), pp. 25–36

—— 'Notas para uma análise metodológica de "O Capital"', *Revista Brasiliense*, 29 (1960), pp. 60–72

—— *Origens da dialética do trabalho: estudo sobre lógica do jovem Marx* (São Paulo: Difel, 1966)

Giblin, James, and Jamie Monson, *Maji Maji: Lifting the Fog of War* (Leiden: Brill, 2010)

Glissant, Édouard, *Poetics of Relation*, trans. by Betsy Wing (Ann Arbor: University of Michigan Press, 1990)

Gonzalez, Lélia, 'A categoria político-cultural de amefricanidade', in *Por um feminismo afro-latino-americano: ensaios, intervenções e diálogos*, ed. by Flávia Rios and Márcia Lima (Rio de Janeiro: Zahar, 2020), pp. 127–38

—— 'Por Um Feminismo Afro-Latino-Americano', in *Por Um Feminismo Afro-Latino-Americano*, ed. by Flavia Rios and Márcia Lima (Rio de Janeiro: Zahar, 1988), pp. 139–50

Green, Nile, *The Persianate World: The Frontiers of a Eurasian Lingua Franca* (Berkeley: University of California Press, 2019)

Gueroult, Martial, *Descartes selon l'ordre des raisons*, 2 vols (Paris: Aubier-Montaigne, 1953)

Haraway, Donna J., *Manifestly Haraway* (Minneapolis: University of Minnesota Press, 2016)

Harlow, Barbara, and Mia Carter, eds, *Archives of Empire*, 2 vols (Durham, NC: Duke University Press, 2003–04), II: *The Scramble for Africa* (2004)

Hartman, Saidiya, *Venus in Two Acts* (New York: Cassandra Press, 2021)

Heinrichs, Katrin, and Hendrik Sonnabend, 'Leaky Pipeline or Glass Ceiling? Empirical Evidence from the German Academic Career Ladder', *Applied Economics Letters*, 2 (2022), pp. 1–5

Held, David, and Thomas Hale, eds, *Handbook of Transnational Governance: New Institutions and Innovations* (Cambridge: Polity Press, 2011)

Heller, Mareike, ed., *No Humboldt 21! — Dekoloniale Einwände gegen das Humboldt-Forum* (Berlin: AfricAvenir International, 2017)

hooks, bell, *Ain't I a Woman: Black Women and Feminism* (Boston: South End Press, 1981)

Horrocks, David, and Eva Kolinsky, eds, *Turkish Culture in German Society Today* (New York: Berghahn, 1996)

Instituto Nacional de Estudos e Pesquisas Educacionais Anísio Teixeira, *Censo da Educação superior — Notas Estatísticas — 2019* (Brasília: Ministério da Educação, 2019)

James, C. L. R., *The Black Jacobins: Toussaint L'Ouverture and the San Domingo Revolution* (New York: Penguin, 2001)

Jameson, Fredric, *Valences of the Dialectic* (London: Verso Books, 2010)

Katouzian, Homa, *Iranian History and Politics: The Dialectic of State and Society* (London: Routledge, 2012)

Katouzian, Homa, and Alireza Korangi, *Poetry and Revolution: The Poets and Poetry of the Constitutional Era of Iran* (London: Taylor & Francis, 2022)

Khatibi, Abdelkebir, *Plural Maghreb: Writings on Postcolonialism*, trans. by P. Burcu Yalim, Suspensions: Contemporary Middle Eastern and Islamicate Thought (London: Bloomsbury Academic, 2019)

Kia, Mana, *Persianate Selves: Memories of Place and Origin before Nationalism* (Redwood City, CA: Stanford University Press, 2020)

Kilomba, Grada, 'Decolonising Knowledge', in *The Struggle Is Not Over Yet: An Archive in Relation*, ed. by Nuno Faria,

Filipa César, and Tobias Hering (Berlin: Archive Books, 2015), pp. 191–208

—— *Plantation Memories: Episodes of Everyday Racism* (Toronto: Between the Lines, 2021)

Koutsoukos, Sandra Sofia Machado, *Zoológicos humanos: gente em exibição na era do imperialismo* (Campinas: Editora da Universidade Estadual de Campinas, 2020)

Lacan, Jacques, *The Four Fundamental Concepts of Psychoanalysis*, ed. by Jacques-Alain Miller, trans. by Alan Sheridan (London: Hogarth Press, 1971)

Laval, Christian, and Pierre Dardot, 'Grande conférence (FQPPU)', online video recording, YouTube, 2017 <https://www.youtube.com/watch?v=LGFpK3LJGGk> [accessed 15 December 2022]

Le Guin, Ursula K., 'The Carrier Bag Theory of Fiction', in *Carrier Bag Fiction*, ed. by Sarah Shin and Matthias Zeiske (Leipzig: Spector Books, 2021), pp. 34–44

—— *The Word for World Is Forest* (New York: TOR, 1972)

Lederman, Josh, 'Corporations Are Turning to Forest Credits in the Race to Go "Carbon-Neutral." Advocates Worry about "Greenwashing"', *NBC News*, 5 December 2021 <https://www.nbcnews.com/news/world/corporations-are-turning-forest-credits-race-go-carbon-neutral-advocat-rcna7259> [accessed 18 December 2022]

Levander, Caroline, and Walter Mignolo, 'Introduction: The Global South and World Dis/Order', *The Global South*, 5.1 (2011), pp. 1–11 <https://doi.org/10.2979/globalsouth.5.1.1>

Lima, Pedro, 'As desventuras do Marxismo: Fernando Henrique Cardoso, antagonismo e reconciliação (1955–1968)' (Doctoral Dissertation, Universidade do Estado do Rio de Janeiro, 2015)

Lindner, Kolja, 'Le Modèle allemand: précarité et résistances dans l'enseignement supérieur et la recherche d'outre-Rhin', in *Liberté de la recherche. Conflits, pratiques, horizons*, ed. by Mélanie Duclos and Anders Fjeld (Paris: Editions Kimäe, 2019), pp. 209–18, available online <https://shs.hal.science/halshs-02496377/document> [accessed 5 October 2023], pp. 1–6

Lorde, Audre, *The Black Unicorn* (New York: Norton and Company, 1995)

Lotze, Birgit, 'Afrikanisches Viertel: Deshalb werden Straßen umbenannt', *Berliner Morgenpost*, 29 November 2022 <https://www.morgenpost.de/bezirke/mitte/article237030899/Wechsel-im-Afrikanischen-Viertel.html> [accessed 14 December 2022]

Lugones, María, 'Heterosexualism and the Colonial/Modern Gender System', *Hypatia*, 22.1 (2007), pp. 186–209

Lukács, György, *History and Class Consciousness: Studies in Marxist Dialectics*, trans. by Rodney Livingstone (Cambridge, MA: MIT Press, 1971)

Martins, Leda Maria, *Afrografias da Memória* (São Paulo, Belo Horizonte: Perspectiva, Mazza Edições, 1997)

Marx, Karl, *Capital: A Critique of Political Economy, Vol I: The Process of Production of Capital*, ed. by Friedrich Engels, trans. by Samuel Moore and Edward Aveling, in *Marx and Engels Collected Works*, 50 vols (London: Lawrence & Wishart, 1975–2004), XXXV (1996)

Marx, Karl, and Frederick Engels, 'Manifesto of the Communist Party', in *Marx/Engels Selected Works*, ed. by Engels (Moscow: Progress Publishers, 1969), pp. 98–137

MasterClass, 'What Does It Mean to Kill Your Darlings?', *MasterClass*, 8 September 2021 <https://www.masterclass.com/articles/what-does-it-mean-to-kill-your-darlings> [accessed 21 December 2022]

Matin-Asgari, Afshin, *Both Eastern and Western: An Intellectual History of Iranian Modernity* (Cambridge: Cambridge University Press, 2018), pp. 190–222

Mbembe, Achille, *Critique de la raison nègre* (Paris: La Découverte, 2013)

McKittrick, Katherine, *Dear Science and Other Stories* (Durham, NC: Duke University Press, 2021)

Mello, Luiz Carlos, *Nise da Silveira. Caminhos de uma psiquiatra rebelde* (Rio de Janeiro: Automática, 2014)

Menon, Dilip M., ed., *Changing Theory: Concepts from the Global South* (Milton Park: Routledge, 2022)

—— 'Thinking about the Global South', in *The Global South and Literature*, ed. by Russell West-Pavlov (Cambridge: Cambridge University Press, 2018), pp. 34–44 <https://doi.org/10.1017/9781108231930.003>

Merkel, Ian, *Terms of Exchange: Brazilian Intellectuals and the French Social Sciences* (Chicago: The University of Chicago Press, 2022)

Mezzadra, Sandro, and Brett Neilson, 'On the Multiple Frontiers of Extraction: Excavating Contemporary Capitalism', *Cultural Studies*, 31.2–3 (2017), pp. 185–204 <https://doi.org/10.1086/345321>

Mignolo, Walter D., *The Darker Side of Western Modernity: Global Futures, Decolonial Options*, Latin America Otherwise: Languages, Empires, Nations (Durham, NC: Duke University Press, 2011)

—— 'Epistemic Disobedience, Independent Thought and Decolonial Freedom', *Theory, Culture & Society*, 26.7–8 (2009), pp. 159–81 <https://doi.org/10.1177/0263276409349275>

—— 'Introduction: Coloniality of Power and de-Colonial Thinking', *Cultural Studies*, 21.2–3 (2007), pp. 155–67 <https://doi.org/10.1080/09502380601162498>

—— *Local Histories/Global Designs: Coloniality, Subaltern Knowledges, and Border Thinking*, Princeton Studies in Culture/Power/History (Princeton, NJ: Princeton University Press, 2012)

Mignolo, Walter, 'Foreword: Yes, We Can', in Hamid Dabashi, *Can Non-Europeans Think?*, pp. viii–xlii

Miguel, Marlon, 'Psychiatric Power: Exclusion and Segregation in the Brazilian Mental Health System', in *Democracy and Brazil: Collapse and Regression*, ed. by Bernardo Bianchi et al. (London: Routledge, 2020), pp. 250–67

Mills, Ivy, 'Sutura: Gendered Honor, Social Death and the Politics of Exposure in Senegalese Literature and Popular Culture' (Doctoral Dissertation, African American Studies, University of California, Berkeley, 2011)

Mombaça, Jota, *Não Vão Nos Matar Agora* (Rio de Janeiro: Cobogó, 2021)

Moore, Jason W., ed., *Anthropocene or Capitalocene?: Nature, History, and the Crisis of Capitalism* (Oakland, CA: PM Press, 2016)

Morat, Daniel, 'Katalysator wider Willen: Das Humboldt Forum in Berlin und die deutsche Kolonialvergangenheit', *Zeithistorische Forschungen — Studies in Contemporary History*, 16

(2019), pp. 140–53 <https://doi.org/10.14765/zzf.dok-1342>

Morgenthaler, Walter, *Ein Geisteskranker als Künstler: Adolf Wölfli* [1921] (Bern: Zentrum Paul Klee, 2021)

Morton, Timothy, *All Art is Ecological* (London: Penguin Books, 2021)

Museum am Rothenbaum — Kulturen und Künste der Welt, 'Hey Hamburg, do you know Duala Manga Bell?', exhibition website: <https://markk-hamburg.de/ausstellungen/hey-hamburg/> [accessed 14 December 2022]

Museum Treptow, Exhibition: '*zurückgeschaut | Looking back*: Die Erste Deutsche Kolonialausstellung von 1896 in Berlin-Treptow' <https://www.berlin.de/museum-treptow-koepenick/ausstellungen/artikel.649851.php> [accessed 3 January 2023]

Nabavi, Negin, *Intellectuals and the State in Iran: Politics, Discourse, and the Dilemma of Authenticity* (Gainesville: University Press of Florida, 2003)

Nascimento, Beatriz, 'Transcrição do Documentário Orí [1989]', in *Beatriz Nascimento. Quilombola e Intelectual. Possibilidade nos Dias da Destruição*, ed. by União dos Coletivos Pan-Africanistas (Diáspora Africana: Editora Filhos da África, 1989), pp. 326–40

Ngũgĩ wa Thiong'o, *Globalectics: Theory and the Politics of Knowing*, The Wellek Library Lectures in Critical Theory (New York: Columbia University Press, 2012)

—— *Secure the Base: Making Africa Visible in the Globe*, The Africa List (London: Seagull Books, 2016)

Novais, Fernando, *Portugal e Brasil na crise do antigo sistema colonial (1777–1808)*, 5th edn (São Paulo: Hucitec, 1989)

Odenthal, Johannes, and Judith Weber, Profile of Mnyaka Sururu Mboro, Koloniales Erbe Project Website, 2018 <https://www.adk.de/de/projekte/2018/koloniales-erbe/symposium-I/teilnehmer/mnyaka-sururu-mboro.htm> [accessed 27 December 2022]

Oestermann, Tristan, *Kautschuk und Arbeit in Kamerun unter deutscher Kolonialherrschaft 1880–1913* (Vienna: Böhlau Verlag, 2023)

Oswald, Margareta von, *Working Through Colonial Collections: 'Africa' in Berlin's Humboldt Forum* (Leuven: Leuven University Press, 2022)

Oury, Jean, 'Psychanalyse, psychiatrie et psychothérapie institutionnelles', *VST — Vie sociale et traitements*, 95 (2007), pp. 110–125 <https://doi.org/10.3917/vst.095.0110>

Pereira, Astrojildo, *Ensaios históricos e políticos*, ed. by Heitor Ferreira Lima (São Paulo: Alfa-Omega, 1979)

Piedalue, Amy, and Susmita Rishi, 'Unsettling the South through Postcolonial Feminist Theory', *Feminist Studies*, 43.3 (2017), pp. 548–70

Pina-Cabral, João de, 'Outros nomes, histórias cruzadas: apresentando o debate', *Etnográfica*, 12.1 (2008), pp. 5–16

Plant, Sadie, *Zeros and Ones: Digital Women and the New Technoculture* (London: Fourth Estate, 1995)

Pons-Vignon, Nicolas, 'Reflections on the Paradox of German Academic Precarity' (Kassel: ICDD, University of Kassel), online video recording, YouTube, 17 December 2019 <https://www.youtube.com/watch?v=c4TMikEHMr4 > [accessed 15 December 2022]

Prado Jr, Caio, *Formação do Brasil contemporâneo* (São Paulo: Companhia das Letras, 2011)

Prebisch, Raúl, 'The Economic Development of Latin America and Its Principal Problems', Economic Commission for Latin America, 1950 <https://repositorio.cepal.org/handle/11362/29973> [accessed 11 February 2023]

Preciado, Beatriz, *Testo Yonqui. Sexo, Droga y Biopolítica* (Barcelona: Espasa, 2008)

Prinzhorn, Hans, *Bildnerei der Geisteskranken* [1922] (Hamburg: Severus Verlag, 2016)

Quashie, Hélène, 'La Blanchité au miroir de l'africanité: migrations et constructions sociales urbaines d'une assignation identitaire peu explorée', *Cahiers d'études africaines*, 220 (2015), pp. 760–85

Quijano, Aníbal, 'Coloniality and Modernity/Rationality', *Cultural Studies*, 21.2–3 (2007), pp. 168–78 <https://doi.org/10.1080/09502380601164353>

—— 'Coloniality of Power and Eurocentrism in Latin America', *International Sociology*, 15.2 (2000), pp. 215–32 <https://doi.org/10.1177/0268580900015002005>

Rahnema, Majid, and Victoria Bawartree, *The Post-development Reader* (London: Zed Books, 1997)

Reid, Don, 'Etienne Balibar: Algeria, Althusser, and Altereuropéenisation', *South Central Review*, 25.3 (2008), pp. 68–85.

Reuters, 'Events in Iran since Mahsa Amini's Arrest and Death in Custody', *Reuters*, 12 December 2022 <https://www.reuters.com/world/middle-east/events-iran-since-mahsa-aminis-arrest-death-custody-2022-10-05/> [accessed 6 February 2023]

Riccio, Bruno, 'Talkin' about Migration: Some Ethnographic Notes on the Ambivalent Representation of Migrants in Contemporary Senegal', *Stichproben — Vienna Journal of African Studies*, 8 (2005), pp. 99–118 <https://stichproben.univie.ac.at/fileadmin/user_upload/p_stichproben/Artikel/Nummer08/07_Riccio.pdf> [accessed 11 March 2020]

Rich, Adrienne, 'Notes Towards a Politics of Location', in *Blood, Bread and Poetry: Selected Prose 1979–1985*, ed. by Adrienne Rich (London: Little Brown and Co.), pp. 211–31

Rivera Cusicanqui, Silvia, *Ch'ixinakax utxiwa: On Practices and Discourses of Decolonization*, trans. Molly Geidel (Cambridge: Polity Press, 2010)

—— *Un mundo ch'ixi es posible. Ensayos desde un presente en crisis* (Buenos Aires: Tinta Limón, 2018)

Robcis, Camille, *Disalienation: Politics, Philosophy, and Radical Psychiatry in Postwar France* (Chicago: The University of Chicago Press, 2021)

Rodrigues Jr, Gilson José, 'Em nome do reino: ações humanitárias brasileiras de Tuparetama (Brasil) a Dakar (Senegal)' (Doctoral Dissertation, Social Anthropology, Centre for Philosophy and Human Sciences, Federal University of Pernambuco, Recife, 2019)

Rodrigues, Lidiane, 'A produção social do marxismo universitário em São Paulo: mestres, discípulos e "um seminário" (1958–1978)' (Doctoral Dissertation, University of São Paulo, 2011)

Rosander, Eva Evers, *In Pursuit of Paradise: Senegalese Women, Muridism and Migration* (Los Angeles: Nordic Africa Institute, 2015)

Rosário, Fernanda, Letícia Filho, and Victor Oliveira, 'O perfil da COP-26 mostra que o debate sobre o clima ainda exclui as mulheres', *Alma preta*, 3 September 2022 <https://almapreta.com.br/sessao/politica/so-macho-perfil-da-cop-mostra-que-o-debate-climatico-ainda-exclui-mulheres/> [accessed 15 December 2022]

Rowland, Robert, 'Práticas de nomeação em Portugal durante a Época moderna — ensaio de aproximação', *Etnográfica*, 12.1 (2008), pp. 17–43

Said, Edward W., *Orientalism* (New York: Pantheon Books, 1978)

—— 'Orientalism Reconsidered', *Cultural Critique*, 1 (1985), pp. 89–107

—— *Reflections on Exile and Other Essays* (Cambridge, MA: Harvard University Press, 2002)

Santos, Boaventura de Sousa, *Decolonising the University: The Challenge of Deep Cognitive Justice* (Newcastle upon Tyne: Cambridge Scholars Publishing, 2018)

—— *Epistemologies of the South: Justice Against Epistemicide* (New York: Routledge, 2014)

Santos dos Santos, Frederico, 'Casa de tèranga: nomeações e materialidades na migração transnacional entre Senegal e Brasil' (Doctoral Dissertation, Social Anthropology, Federal University of São Carlos, São Carlos, 2022)

Sartre, Jean-Paul, *Search for a Method*, trans. by Hazel Barnes (New York: Alfred A. Knopf, 1963)

Schmidlehner, Michael, 'Banco de Códigos da Amazônia', in *Uwa'Kürü: dicionário analítico*, ed. by Gerson de Albuquerque and Agenor Pacheco (Rio Branco: Edufac & Nepan Editora, 2020), pp. 28–37

Schwarcz, Lilia Moritz, *O espetáculo das raças: cientistas, instituições e questão racial no Brasil. 1870–1930* (São Paulo: Companhia das Letras, 2005), pp. 189–238

Schwarz, Roberto, 'As Ideias fora do lugar', in *Ao Vencedor as Batatas* (São Paulo: Editora 34, 2000)

—— *A Master on the Periphery of Capitalism: Machado de Assis*, trans. by John Gledson, Post-Contemporary Interventions (Durham, NC: Duke University Press, 2001)

—— 'Sobre a leitura de Marx no Brasil', in *Nós que amávamos tanto 'O Capital'*, ed. by Emir Sader et al. (São Paulo: Boitempo, 2017), para. 1–17

—— *To the Victor, the Potatoes!: Literary Form and Social Process in the Beginnings of the Brazilian Novel*, ed. and trans. by Ronald W. Sousa (Leiden: Brill, 2019)

—— 'Um seminário de Marx', in *Sequências brasileiras: ensaios* (São Paulo: Companhia das Letras, 1999), pp. 86–105

Scott, David, *Conscripts of Modernity: The Tragedy of Colonial Enlightenment* (Durham, NC: Duke University Press, 2004)

Sebald, Peter, *Die deutsche Kolonie Togo 1884–1914: Auswirkungen einer Fremdherrschaft* (Berlin: C. Links, 2013)

Segato, Rita Laura, and Ramsey McGlazer, *The Critique of Coloniality: Eight Essays* (New York: Routledge, 2022)

Silveira, Nise da, '20 anos de Terapêutica Ocupacional em Engenho de Dentro', *Revista Brasileira de Saúde Mental*, 10 (1966), pp. 17–160

—— *Cartas a Spinoza* (Rio de Janeiro: Francisco Alves, 1995)

—— *Casa das Palmeiras: a emoção de lidar, uma experiência em psiquiatria* (Rio de Janeiro: Alhambra, 1986)

—— *Imagens do Inconsciente* (Rio de Janeiro: Alhambra, 1981)

—— 'Nise da Silveira, Artaud e Jung', interview with David Bocai et al. for *Rádice* (1976–77), in Luiz Carlos Mello, *Encontros/Nise da Silveira* (Rio de Janeiro: Azougue, 2009), pp. 44–75

—— 'O mundo contemporâneo é impaciente', interview with Luiz Carlos Lisboa, *O Estado de São Paulo*, newspaper online archive, 24 January 1987, p. 58 <https://acervo.estadao.com.br/> [accessed 1 February 2023]

—— *Os inumeráveis estados do ser* (Rio de Janeiro: Museu de Imagens do Inconsciente, 1987)

Statistisches Bundesamt, 'Personal an Hochschulen 2016' <https://www.destatis.de/DE/Themen/Gesellschaft-Umwelt/Bildung-Forschung-Kultur/Hochschulen/Publikationen/Downloads-Hochschulen/personal-vorbericht-5213402168004.pdf?__blob=publicationFile> [accessed 15 December 2022]

Statistisches Bundesamt, 'Zahl der Habilitationen 2017 gegenüber Vorjahr geringfügig um 0,3 % gestiegen' <https://www.destatis.de/DE/Presse/Pressemitteilungen/2018/07/PD18_242_213.html> [accessed 15 December 2022]

Streva, Juliana M., 'Fugitive Dialogues: Speaking Nearby Lélia Gonzalez and Frantz Fanon', *Philosophy and Global Affairs Journal* (forthcoming, 2024)

Streva, Juliana M., Ana Luiza Braga, and Lior Zalis, 'Speculating Pacts on the Common', *La Escuela* (2022) <https://laescuela.art/en/campus/library/mappings/speculating-pacts-on-the-common-ana-luiza-braga-juliana-streva-and-lior-zisman-zalis>

Sunseri, Thaddeus, 'The Maji-Maji War, 1905–1907', in *Oxford Research Encyclopedia of African History*, ed. by Thomas Spear (Oxford: Oxford University Press, 2022), pp. 1–40 <https://doi.org/10.1093/acrefore/9780190277734.013.154>

Tavakoli-Targhi, Mohammad, 'Early Persianate Modernity', in *Forms of Knowledge in Early Modern Asia: Explorations in the Intellectual History of India and Tibet, 1500–1800*, ed. by Sheldon Pollock (Durham, NC: Duke University Press, 2011), pp. 257–87

—— *Refashioning Iran: Orientalism, Occidentalism and Historiography* (London: Palgrave, 2001)

'Theorizing Through the Global South', workshop, ICI Berlin, 10–11 March 2022 <https://doi.org/10.25620/e220310>

Thiemeyer, Thomas, 'Cosmopolitanizing Colonial Memories in Germany', *Critical Inquiry*, 45 (2019), pp. 967–90 <https://doi.org/10.1086/703964>

Tosquelles, François, *Soigner les institutions* (Paris: L'Arachnéen, 2021)

Towfigh, Ebrahim, and Shirin Ahmadnia, 'How to Overcome "Oriental" Sociology?', in *Spatial Social Thought: Local Knowledge in Global Science Encounters*, ed. by Michael Kuhn (New York: Columbia University Press, 2014), pp. 313–26

Trinh T. Minh-ha, '"Speaking Nearby": A Conversation with Trinh T. Minh-ha', *Visual Anthropology Review*, 8.1 (1992), pp. 82–91

—— *When the Moon Waxes Red: Representation, Gender and Cultural Politics* (New York: Routledge, 1991)

—— *Woman, Native, Other: Writing Postcoloniality and Feminism* (Bloomington: Indiana University Press, 1989)

Trinh T. Minh-ha, and Stanley Gray, 'The Plural Void: Barthes and Asia', *SubStance*, 11.3 (1982), pp. 41–50 <https://doi.org/10.2307/3684313>

Tsing, Anna L., *The Mushroom at the End of the World: On the Possibilities of Life in Capitalist Ruins* (Princeton, NJ: Princeton University Press, 2015)

United Nations Development Programme, Special issue 'Forging a Global South', United Nations Day for South-South Cooperation, 19 December 2004

Université Ouverte, 'La Précarité dans l'enseignement et la recherche', 10 February 2020 <https://universiteouverte.org/2020/02/10/la-precarite-dans-lenseignement-et-la-recherche/> [accessed 15 May 2023]

Verburgt, Lukas M., 'The History of Knowledge and the Future History of Ignorance', *KNOW: A Journal on the Formation of Knowledge*, 4.1 (2020), p. 5 <https://doi.org/10.1086/708341>.

Vereinigung der Kanzlerinnen und Kanzler der Universitäten Deutschlands, 'Bayreuther Erklärung zu befristeten Beschäftigungsverhältnissen mit wissenschaftlichem und künstlerischem Personal in Universitäten', September 2019 <https://www.uni-kanzler.de/fileadmin/user_upload/05_Publikationen/2017_-_2010/20190919_Bayreuther_Erklaerung_der_Universitaetskanzler_final.pdf> [accessed 15 December 2022]

Vinchon, Jean, *L'Art et la folie* (Paris: Stock, 1924)

Walsh, Catherine E., 'The Decolonial For: Resurgences, Shifts, and Movements', in *On Decoloniality: Concepts, Analytics, Praxis*, ed. by Walter Mignolo and Catherine E. Walsh (Durham, NC: Duke University Press, 2018), pp. 15–32

Welcomed to Germany?, dir. by Özlem Sarıyıldız (Utopictures, 2018)

Werneck Sodré, Nelson, *Capitalismo e revolução burguesa no Brasil* (Belo Horizonte: Nossa Terra, 1990)

Worringer, Wilhelm, *Abstraction and Empathy: A Contribution to the Psychology of Style*, trans. by Michael Bullock Eastford (CT: Martino Fine Books, 2014)

Wynter, Sylvia, 'Unsettling the Coloniality of Being/Power/Truth/Freedom: Towards the Human, After Man, its Overrepresentation — An Argument', *CR: The New Centennial Review*, 3.3 (2003), pp. 257–337 <https://doi.org/10.1353/ncr.2004.0015>

Notes on the Contributors

Mahmoud Al-Zayed is a literary scholar of comparative and world literatures, working across different theoretical and literary traditions with a focus on south-south affinities and connections across South Asia, Africa(na), and the Arab and Islamicate World. He works at the intersections of anticolonial, postcolonial, and decolonial traditions of thought and practice. He writes on activism, aesthetics, ethics, decolonisation, philosophies of liberation, and intellectual history and social theory from contemporary Arab and Muslim thought. He is a post-doctoral research associate and an Einstein Researcher at the Institute of Islamic Studies, and Berlin Graduate School Muslim Cultures and Societies, Freie Universität Berlin. Al-Zayed studied English language and Literature in Homs, Syria, and before moving to Berlin, he spent the last decade studying and researching as an Indian Council for Cultural Relations fellow, at Jamia Millia Islamia, a Central University, New Delhi, India.

Bernardo Bianchi is a visiting professor at the University of São Paulo. He serves as a researcher at the Centre Marc Bloch in Berlin, where he coordinates the Alexander von Humboldt project 'Paradoxes of Emancipation'. Prior to this, he held post-doctoral fellowships at the Freie Universität Berlin and the Goethe-Universität Frankfurt am Main. He co-edited the volume *Materialism and Politics*, published by ICI Berlin Press in 2021. His primary research interests include Political Philosophy, History of Philosophy, and Contemporary Political Theory.

Michela Coletta is an Assistant Professor in Hispanic Studies at the University of Warwick. She is currently Marie Curie Fellow in Global History at Freie Universität Berlin and an Affiliated Fellow at ICI Berlin (2022–24). She has a PhD in History from University College London and has held positions at King's College London, the University of Bristol, the University of London's

Centre for Latin American and Caribbean Studies, and the Universidad Pablo de Olavide. She has also been a Visiting Scholar at the University of Aalborg and at the Rachel Carson Center. Coletta's first monograph, *Decadent Modernity: Civilisation and Latinidad in Spanish America, 1880–1920* (2018), shows the relevance of cultural frameworks of modernity in the emergence of Latin America as a geo-political region. She has also co-edited the volume *Provincialising Nature: Multidisciplinary Approaches to the Politics of the Environment in Latin America* (2016) and has published several articles at the intersection of cultural and intellectual history, environmental history, social and political theory, and the environmental humanities. Her current work on Buen Vivir explores the possibility of tracing anti-extractivist epistemologies across north-south boundaries.

Iracema Dulley works as an anthropologist, psychoanalyst, and creative writer. She holds a BA in philosophy and a PhD in social anthropology from the University of São Paulo and is currently Research Fellow at the Institute of Social Sciences of the University of Lisbon. Her research considers processes of subject constitution from an interdisciplinary perspective. She is the author of books including *On the Emic Gesture* (Routledge, 2019), *Os nomes dos outros* (Humanitas, 2015), and *Deus é feiticeiro* (Annablume, 2010). Recent publications include: 'Naming Others: Translation and Subject Constitution in the Central Highlands of Angola (1926–1961)' in *Comparative Studies in Society and History*, Vol. 64, Issue 2 (April 2022), pp. 363–93; 'Chronicles of Bailundo: A Fragmentary Account in Umbundu of Life Before and After Portuguese Colonial Rule' in *Africa*, Vol. 91, Issue 5 (November 2021), pp. 713–41; 'The Voice in Rape', in *European Journal of Psychoanalysis*, Vol. 9, Issue 2 (2022); 'Feitiço/Umbanda', in *Changing Theory: Concepts from the Global South*, ed. Dilip Menon (Routledge, 2022); and 'The Case and the Signifier: Generalization in Freud's Rat Man', in *The Case for Reduction*, ed. Christopher Holzhey and Jakob Schillinger (ICI Berlin Press, 2022).

Şirin Fulya Erensoy is a film and media scholar, based between Istanbul and Berlin. Her research focuses on video activism, women and documentary filmmaking, and genre cinema. She has experience as a lecturer in Film and Television at various institutions in Turkey and recently completed her Marie Curie Individual post-doctoral fellowship at the Film University Babelsberg Konrad Wolf (September 2021–August 2023). She supplements her academic work with ongoing practices in documentary film production, film curation, and journalism. Şirin has curated numerous art and film events in cooperation with institutions in Berlin, including the Maxim Gorki Theatre, and the Kunstraum Kreuzberg/Bethanien and has been involved in festivals such as the Hive International Short Film Days and the Sehsüchte International Student Film Festival. Her professional journey also includes her role as anchor for the English news-bulletin 'This Week' in Turkey on the alternative digital media platform Medyascope TV. In addition to her roles in media and academia, Erensoy has worked on international film projects in various capacities such as editing, producing, translating, and researching. Furthermore, she has directed her own short films and videos, some of which have received funding from the Ministry of Culture and Tourism of Turkey, the Turkish Foundation of Cinema and Audiovisual Culture, and Goethe Institut Istanbul.

Firoozeh Farvardin is a feminist scholar and sociologist based in Berlin. She is researching and writing on gender/sexual (counter)strategies of authoritarian neoliberalism in Iran as a postdoc fellow at IRGAC (International Research Group on Authoritarianism and Counter Strategy), Rosa Luxemburg Foundation, hosted by the Humboldt University of Berlin. She is also a MERGE (Migration and the Middle East Research Network) affiliated researcher and a guest lecturer at the Berlin Institute for Integration and Migration Research (BIM), where her research revolves around the intersection of mobility and mobilization, as well as knowledge production about and from the Middle East. In 2023, she co-curated an internationalist gathering of feminist movements and scholars from the Global South in Berlin: 'Beyond Equality: Feminisms Reclaiming Life', hosted by the HAU (Hebbel am Ufer) theatre and performance center. She is currently working on her first monograph on the emergence of neoliberal gender/sexual politics in Iran.

Özgün Eylül İşcen is a media art theorist, lecturer, and curator based in Berlin and an affiliated fellow at the ICI Berlin. She holds a PhD in Computational Media, Arts, and Cultures from

Duke University (2020). Her research focuses on the geopolitical aesthetic of computational media by delving into media histories and arts within the context of the Middle East. She is currently part of the research team *Against Catastrophe* led by Prof. Orit Halpern based at Technische Universität Dresden. She also co-edits web-based publishing *Counter-N* with Prof. Shintaro Miyazaki based at Humboldt-Universität zu Berlin. Her recent publications include: 'The Racial Politics of Smart Urbanism: Dubai and Beirut as Two Sides of the Same Coin', in *Special Issue: The Politics of Race and Racialisation in the Middle East*, ed. by Burcu Özçelik; *Ethnic and Racial Studies*, 44:12, 2282–2303, 2021; 'Black Box Allegories of Gulf Futurism: The Irreducible Other of Computational Capital,' in *The Case for Reduction*, ed. by Christoph F. E. Holzhey and Jakob Schillinger (ICI Berlin Press, 2022).

Kata Katz is a lecturer and PhD Candidate at the University of Arts Berlin, Germany. She studied philosophy, literature, and films studies at the University of Szeged, Hungary. Exploring how the photographic medium is used to construct different realities through its social and scientific uses, her research focuses on the connection between performativity and photography at the intersection of gender, sexuality, race, class and age. She has co-authored several essays that explore the benefits of failure in academia and beyond, as well as the future realities of science and research in the Danube region.

Bruna Martins Coelho is an associate researcher at the Centre Marc Bloch, having obtained her doctorate in philosophy from the University of Paris 8 in 2022, with the thesis titled 'The Making of the Traditional Brazilian Family: An Obituary of the Brazilian Nation' (with funding from Brazilian Ministry of Education/CAPES). In this genealogical study, she investigates the mutations of familial nationalism in Brazil, analyzing the interconnection between whiteness, rape, and the construction of the national political body. She is a member of the 'Paradoxes of Emancipation: Knowledge and Democracy in the Post-Truth Era' project (Centre Marc Bloch/Humboldt, University of São Paulo) and of the Nexos-Southeast research group (Cnpq/Brazil). She has taught as a lecturer at the European University Viadrina Frankfurt (Oder) (2023) and at the University of Toulouse Jean-Jaurès (2019). Her research, markedly transdisciplinary, is situated at the boundary between political philosophy, feminist and decolonial epistemologies, history, and French post-structuralism. She has also participated in the organization of activities to combat gender violence: the design of the cultural mediation project at the São Paulo Cultural Center signed by the GENERX collective (2015) and the Faire Face association workshops in Toulouse (2016-2017).

Marlon Miguel is the Co-Principal Investigator at the project 'Madness, Media, Milieus. Reconfiguring the Humanities in Postwar Europe' at Bauhaus-Universität Weimar. He holds a double PhD in Fine Arts (Université Paris 8 Vincennes-Saint-Denis) and Philosophy (Federal University of Rio de Janeiro). His current research focuses on the intersection between contemporary philosophy, art, anthropology, and psychiatry. He also practices contemporary circus and does practical movement research. His recent publications include *Camering: Fernand Deligny On Cinema and the Image* (Leiden University Press, 2022); 'Representing the World, Weathering Its End. Arthur Bispo do Rosário's Ecology of the Ship' in *Weathering: Ecologies of Exposure* ed. by Christoph F. E. Holzhey Arnd Wedemeyer (ICI Berlin Press, 2020; republished in *Afterall*, 54, 2023); and 'La clinique de Nise da Silveira au croisement de la psychanalyse, de la psychothérapie institutionnelle et des révolutions psychiatriques' in *Psychanalyse du reste du monde: Géo-histoire d'une subversion* (La Découverte, 2023).

Frederico Santos dos Santos has a BA (2000) and MA (2005) in Social Sciences from the Pontifical Catholic University of Rio Grande do Sul and a PhD in Social Anthropology from the Federal University of São Carlos (2022). He is a professor at the Institute of Humanities, Sciences, Education and Creativity at the University of Passo Fundo (IHCEC/UPF), Brazil, where he acts as an advisor in the development of policies of affirmative action for black and indigenous people. He has carried out fieldwork and ethnographic research in Senegal and Brazil, addressing the transnational changes of Senegalese migrants between these two countries. He has published on ethnic and racial relations, migration, and their intersections with religion, nationality, class, and race.

Ana Carolina Schveitzer is currently a PhD student in African History at the Department for African Studies at Humboldt Universität zu Berlin. She studied at the Federal University of Santa Catarina (Brazil), where she earned an MA in History (2016) and a BA in History (2014). Her research highlights the connections between photography, work, and colonialism in Africa. She focuses on how German colonialism employed photography in Africa and how the circulation and production of photographs established broader links with the colonial system. Adopting a Visual History approach, her project aims to comprehend a colonial photographic standard related to the theme of work. The project is financially supported by the Deutscher Akademischer Austauschdienst, the German Historical Institut of London, and Stiftung Bildung und Wissenschaft.

Juliana M. Streva is a transdisciplinary researcher and film-maker, with a background in law and critical legal studies. She currently works as a postdoctoral associate at the Institutes of Latin American Studies and Sociology at Freie Universität Berlin, as a member at the research consortium 'Beyond Social Cohesion: Global Repertoires of Living Together' (RePLITO), funded by Berlin University Alliance. Previously, she was a postdoctoral fellow at the Maria Sibylla Merian Centre Conviviality-Inequality in Latin America (Mecila), and a visiting fellow at the Universidade de São Paulo, Hebrew University of Jerusalem, and Brown University. She has authored a monograph titled *Corpo, Raça, Poder: Extermínio Negro no Brasil* (2018), which addresses the legal-political and onto-epistemological dimensions of the afterlives of slavery and anti-Black violence in Brazil. She directed and produced the films *Mulheres em Movimento* (2020) and *Quilombo, Continuum* (2023). Her work engages with critical black studies, anticolonial epistemologies, queer and feminist theories, with a particular focus on processes of abolition, unmastering, and worldmaking.

Nader Talebi is a postdoctoral researcher at Humboldt University of Berlin, working on migration and revolution in the Middle East with a specific focus on Iran. Since 2015, he has taught there and worked as a mixed-method researcher for several research projects at the Berlin Institute of Migration and Integration Research (BIM). His research interests comprise state theory, migration, revolution, nationalism, racism and politics of knowledge production on/in the Middle East. Born and raised in Iran, he studied software engineering at Iran University of Science and Technology and sociology at Allameh Tabatabai University before receiving his PhD in sociology from Lancaster University in the United Kingdom. He is a former post-doctoral researcher at the University of Mannheim's Center for European Social Research (MZES) and a co-founder and current project leader of MERGE, a research network at BIM bringing together critical scholars working on the Middle East.

Index

Cultural Inquiry

EDITED BY CHRISTOPH F. E. HOLZHEY
AND MANUELE GRAGNOLATI

Milton Keynes UK
Ingram Content Group UK Ltd.
UKHW022153040424
440664UK00008B/82/J